Energy Prosumers: Decentralized Energy Systems for Climate Change, Renewable Energy, Energy Storage, Net Zero, and Smart Grid Solutions

I0040400

Copyright

Energy Prosumers: Decentralized Energy Systems for Climate Change, Renewable Energy, Energy Storage, Net Zero, and Smart Grid Solutions

ISBN (eBook): 978-1-991369-77-2

ISBN (Paperback): 978-1-991369-78-9

Published by Global Climate Solutions

First Edition, 2025

Cover design and interior layout by Global Climate Solutions

Table of Contents

Introduction

Chapter 1: The Foundations of Energy Prosumption

Chapter 2: Technologies Empowering Prosumers

Chapter 3: Policy and Regulatory Frameworks for Prosumers

Chapter 4: Economic and Social Impacts of Prosumers

Chapter 5: The Role of Energy Communities

Chapter 6: Digitalization and the Future of Energy Prosumers

Chapter 7: Prosumers and the Energy Transition

Chapter 8: Challenges and Barriers for Prosumers

Chapter 9: The Path Forward for Energy Prosumers

Conclusion

Introduction

The global energy landscape is undergoing a profound transformation. At the heart of this change is the emergence of *energy prosumers*—individuals and organizations that produce, consume, and sometimes share or sell energy, typically from renewable sources. This shift is not just about technology; it represents a new paradigm in how energy is generated, distributed, and utilized. As traditional, centralized energy systems give way to more decentralized and participatory models, prosumers are becoming key drivers of sustainability, innovation, and resilience in the face of climate change.

In this chapter, we will explore the concept of energy prosumers, tracing their rise in the broader context of energy market evolution and technological advancement. We will highlight their significance in achieving global sustainability goals and emphasize their role in creating a cleaner, more equitable energy future. By setting the stage for the chapters ahead, this introduction provides a foundational understanding of why energy prosumers are central to transforming the energy sector and what lies ahead in their journey.

Definition of Energy Prosumers

Energy prosumers are individuals, businesses, or communities that actively produce, consume, and sometimes share or sell energy, typically generated from renewable sources such as solar, wind, or biomass. The term "prosumer" merges the words "producer" and "consumer," signifying a shift from traditional passive energy consumption to active participation in energy generation and management. Prosumers play a dual role in the energy system by generating their own electricity—often through small-scale renewable energy installations—while also consuming energy from the grid when necessary.

This concept is rooted in the growing decentralization of energy systems, enabled by advances in renewable energy technologies, digital tools, and energy storage solutions. Prosumers are not limited to individuals; they also include energy communities and cooperatives that collectively generate and manage energy resources for local benefit.

Energy prosumers contribute to sustainability by reducing reliance on fossil fuels, lowering greenhouse gas emissions, and promoting energy independence. Their participation in energy markets is also reshaping how electricity is distributed, priced, and consumed. As a result, energy prosumers are emerging as key players in the global transition towards more resilient and sustainable energy systems, reflecting a broader societal shift toward localized, participatory energy production.

Evolution of the Energy Market and the Rise of Prosumers

The energy market has undergone significant transformation over the past few decades, shifting from centralized, fossil fuel-based systems to more decentralized and renewable energy-focused models. Historically, energy generation was dominated by large utility companies operating on a one-directional model, where electricity flowed from power plants to consumers via extensive grid networks. This traditional system emphasized efficiency through scale but limited participation to passive consumption.

The transition towards renewable energy has disrupted this centralized structure. Advances in technology, including solar panels, wind turbines, and energy storage solutions, have made small-scale, distributed energy generation both feasible and affordable. As costs for these technologies decreased, households, businesses, and communities began generating their own electricity. Simultaneously, the integration of smart grids, digital tools, and IoT devices has enabled more interactive and efficient energy management, empowering consumers to become energy producers.

This rise of energy prosumers marks a shift towards a participatory energy model. Prosumers now contribute directly to the energy market by generating, consuming, and sometimes selling excess energy back to the grid or through peer-to-peer trading platforms. This evolution signifies not only technological progress but also a fundamental change in how society approaches energy sustainability and resilience.

Role of Decentralized Energy Systems in Modern Societies

Decentralized energy systems are transforming how societies generate, distribute, and consume energy, playing a crucial role in addressing modern energy challenges. Unlike centralized systems, where large power plants feed electricity into extensive grid networks, decentralized systems rely on smaller, localized energy sources such as solar panels, wind turbines, and microgrids. These systems are often situated close to the point of consumption, reducing transmission losses and enhancing overall energy efficiency.

In modern societies, decentralized energy systems contribute to energy security and resilience. By diversifying energy sources and reducing reliance on centralized grids, they minimize vulnerabilities to large-scale disruptions, such as natural disasters or cyberattacks. Additionally, they empower individuals, businesses, and communities to become active participants in energy production, fostering energy independence and reducing reliance on fossil fuels.

These systems also play a vital role in accelerating the transition to renewable energy. They enable greater integration of renewable sources into the energy mix, helping societies meet climate targets and reduce greenhouse gas emissions. Furthermore, decentralized systems promote energy equity by providing access to clean energy in remote or underserved regions, bridging gaps in traditional energy infrastructure and fostering a more inclusive and sustainable energy future.

Importance of Energy Prosumers in Achieving Sustainability Goals

Energy prosumers are critical to advancing sustainability goals by actively contributing to the transition toward cleaner, more resilient energy systems. By generating energy from renewable sources such as solar or wind, prosumers reduce dependence on fossil fuels, thereby lowering greenhouse gas emissions and mitigating climate change. Their role in decentralized energy production also supports the broader adoption of renewable energy technologies, accelerating progress toward international climate targets.

Prosumers contribute to energy efficiency by producing energy closer to where it is consumed, minimizing transmission losses common in centralized systems. They also enable the optimization of energy demand through tools like smart meters and energy management platforms, which reduce waste and improve overall system performance. Furthermore, prosumers often engage in energy sharing or peer-to-peer trading, fostering community-driven energy solutions that align with circular economy principles.

In addition to environmental benefits, prosumers enhance energy equity by enabling localized energy generation in underserved areas, providing greater access to affordable, clean energy. Their participation fosters innovation, drives investment in sustainable technologies, and shifts societal attitudes toward energy as a shared resource rather than a commodity. Ultimately, energy prosumers are central to achieving a sustainable energy future by supporting environmental, economic, and social dimensions of sustainability.

Overview of the Book Structure

This book explores the transformative role of energy prosumers in reshaping the global energy landscape and advancing sustainability. It is structured to provide a comprehensive understanding of energy prosumers, their technologies, challenges, and opportunities, guiding readers through the key elements of this dynamic shift.

The introduction lays the foundation by defining energy prosumers, tracing their rise within the evolving energy market, and explaining their importance in achieving a sustainable future. The first chapter delves deeper into the historical, technological, and economic factors that have enabled the emergence of prosumers.

Chapters two and three focus on the technologies and policies shaping prosumer engagement. Readers will explore innovations like renewable energy systems, smart grids, and digital platforms, alongside the regulatory frameworks supporting their integration into energy markets.

Chapters four through six examine the broader impacts of prosumers, from their economic and social implications to their role in energy communities and the future of decentralized systems. Finally, chapters seven through nine discuss challenges and pathways forward, offering strategies for scaling prosumer adoption, leveraging technological advancements, and fostering global collaboration.

The book concludes with a forward-looking perspective on the potential of energy prosumers to drive sustainable, equitable energy transitions in the years ahead.

Chapter 1: The Foundations of Energy Prosumption

This chapter explores the transformative rise of energy prosumers in the global energy landscape, examining the historical, technological, and economic developments that have enabled prosumer-driven systems. It defines prosumers and their role in decentralized energy networks, tracing the transition from centralized, fossil fuel-based systems to renewable, distributed models. The chapter highlights technological advancements, such as affordable solar panels and smart grids, that empower individuals, businesses, and communities to generate their own energy, while addressing economic factors like declining renewable technology costs and policy incentives driving prosumer adoption. Together, these insights reveal the forces shaping energy prosumption and its impact on transforming the energy sector.

1.1. Understanding Prosumers

The term "prosumer" originated from the merging of "producer" and "consumer," first conceptualized in the 1980s to describe individuals who take an active role in producing goods or services they consume. In the energy sector, this term has gained prominence to define entities—individuals, businesses, or communities—that both produce and consume energy, often through renewable sources. The application of the term in the energy domain reflects a significant shift from traditional, centralized energy systems dominated by utility companies to a more participatory model. Prosumers actively contribute to the generation of electricity, typically using technologies like rooftop solar panels, small wind turbines, or biomass systems. They also engage in energy storage and management, sometimes feeding surplus energy back into the grid.

Energy prosumers are distinguished by several key characteristics that set them apart from traditional energy consumers. First, they actively participate in energy generation, using small-scale renewable energy technologies tailored to meet their specific needs.

Second, prosumers often utilize advanced energy management systems, including smart meters and energy storage devices, to optimize their consumption and production. Third, many prosumers engage in peer-to-peer energy trading, sharing surplus electricity with neighbors or selling it back to the grid, thus contributing to the broader energy network.

One of the most defining roles of energy prosumers is their ability to decentralize energy systems. By producing electricity close to the point of consumption, prosumers reduce reliance on large-scale, centralized power plants and the extensive grid infrastructure required to distribute energy. This decentralization not only improves energy efficiency by minimizing transmission losses but also enhances system resilience. Localized energy production allows communities to better withstand disruptions caused by natural disasters or grid failures, contributing to energy security.

Energy prosumers also play a critical role in advancing sustainability goals. Their use of renewable energy technologies directly reduces greenhouse gas emissions and decreases reliance on fossil fuels. Prosumers embody the transition to clean energy, supporting national and international climate targets. Furthermore, by adopting renewable technologies, prosumers drive demand for innovation, which in turn reduces the costs of these technologies and makes them more accessible to a wider audience.

Another key role of prosumers lies in empowering communities. Through collective projects, such as shared solar farms or community wind turbines, prosumers create opportunities for local collaboration and shared economic benefits. This fosters energy equity by enabling access to renewable energy for those who may not have the resources to invest individually. Additionally, prosumers are reshaping traditional energy markets by introducing competition and innovation, challenging the dominance of utility companies, and creating opportunities for new business models.

1.2. Historical Context

The evolution of energy systems from centralized to decentralized models has marked a pivotal transformation in how energy is generated, distributed, and consumed. Traditionally, energy systems were designed around centralized power plants that produced electricity and transmitted it over extensive grids to consumers. These systems, dominated by fossil fuels, relied on economies of scale to ensure cost-effectiveness and reliability. However, their centralized nature also created vulnerabilities, such as grid failures, transmission losses, and limited adaptability to local energy needs.

The shift toward decentralized energy systems began with the growing awareness of the environmental impacts of fossil fuel-based energy production and the increasing affordability of renewable energy technologies. Decentralized systems rely on localized energy generation, such as solar panels, wind turbines, and small-scale hydropower, which produce energy closer to the point of consumption. This reduces transmission losses and allows for more resilient energy networks, particularly in areas prone to natural disasters or energy insecurity. Decentralization empowers individuals and communities to take an active role in energy production, laying the foundation for the rise of prosumers.

Several milestones in renewable energy adoption have played a critical role in enabling prosumer participation. The 1970s oil crises highlighted the risks of overreliance on fossil fuels, spurring investment in alternative energy sources. During the 1990s and early 2000s, advancements in solar photovoltaic (PV) technology significantly reduced the cost of solar panels, making them accessible to households and businesses. Similarly, improvements in wind turbine efficiency and energy storage technologies expanded the potential for small-scale renewable energy systems. These developments shifted renewable energy from niche applications to mainstream adoption.

The introduction of supportive policies and incentives further accelerated renewable energy adoption. Feed-in tariffs, which guarantee payments to renewable energy producers for feeding electricity into the grid, encouraged individuals and businesses to invest in solar and wind installations. Net metering policies allowed prosumers to offset their energy consumption by exporting surplus energy, creating a financial incentive for small-scale energy production. These policy measures, combined with falling technology costs, created a fertile environment for prosumers to thrive.

Another significant milestone was the development of smart grid technologies, which revolutionized energy management. Smart meters, sensors, and digital platforms enabled real-time monitoring and control of energy consumption and production. These tools allowed prosumers to optimize their energy use, store surplus energy, and even participate in peer-to-peer energy trading. The integration of digital technology into energy systems further democratized energy markets, making it easier for prosumers to engage in decentralized energy production.

1.3. Technology Enablers

The rise of energy prosumers has been made possible by significant technological advancements that enable individuals and communities to generate, store, and manage energy effectively. Among these innovations, solar panels, wind turbines, battery storage, smart grids, and the Internet of Things (IoT) play a central role in transforming traditional energy systems into decentralized, participatory networks.

Solar panels have been a cornerstone technology in the prosumer movement. Over the past few decades, the cost of solar PV systems has decreased dramatically due to advancements in manufacturing processes, material efficiency, and economies of scale. This cost reduction has made solar energy more accessible to households, businesses, and communities. Solar panels offer a flexible solution for small-scale energy production, as they can be installed on rooftops, open spaces, or community-owned land. By converting sunlight into electricity, solar PV systems allow prosumers to reduce their dependence on centralized grids and fossil fuels, contributing to cleaner and more sustainable energy systems.

Wind turbines, particularly small-scale models, are another important technology for prosumers. While traditionally associated with large-scale wind farms, advancements in turbine design have led to the development of compact, efficient turbines suitable for individual or community use. Small wind turbines are often deployed in rural or windy regions where consistent airflow ensures reliable energy generation. These systems complement solar energy by providing electricity during periods of low sunlight, creating a balanced renewable energy mix for prosumers.

Battery storage systems are a critical enabler of prosumer participation by addressing the intermittency challenges of renewable energy. Solar panels and wind turbines generate electricity based on weather conditions, which may not align with energy demand. Battery storage solutions, such as lithium-ion and emerging solid-state batteries, allow prosumers to store excess energy for use during periods of low production or high demand. These systems enhance energy independence and optimize self-consumption, reducing reliance on the grid. Additionally, advanced battery systems enable prosumers to participate in grid balancing by supplying stored energy during peak demand, supporting overall energy system stability.

Smart grids have revolutionized energy management by facilitating two-way communication between energy producers, consumers, and utilities. Unlike traditional grids, which operate on a one-directional flow of electricity, smart grids integrate digital technologies to monitor, control, and optimize energy production and consumption in real time. For prosumers, smart grids enable greater efficiency and participation in the energy system. For instance, smart meters allow users to track energy usage and production, providing insights to improve efficiency. Additionally, smart grids support net metering and peer-to-peer energy trading, where prosumers can sell surplus energy to neighbors or back to the grid, creating economic incentives for renewable energy adoption.

The IoT further enhances prosumer engagement by connecting energy devices and systems for seamless communication and automation. IoT-enabled devices, such as smart thermostats, appliances, and energy management systems, provide prosumers with greater control over their energy use. For example, IoT devices can automatically adjust energy consumption based on real-time data, such as weather conditions or electricity prices, optimizing both energy savings and system performance. In combination with smart grids, IoT enables demand-side management, where energy consumption patterns are aligned with production, reducing strain on the grid and promoting renewable energy integration.

IoT also facilitates the creation of virtual power plants (VPPs), where prosumers collectively contribute their excess energy to create a distributed energy network. VPPs use IoT technology to aggregate energy from multiple prosumers and distribute it efficiently, mimicking the role of a traditional power plant. This model increases the scalability of prosumer participation and strengthens the resilience of decentralized energy systems.

1.4. Economic Drivers

The growth of energy prosumers has been fueled significantly by economic factors that have made renewable energy technologies more accessible and financially viable. Cost reductions in renewable energy technologies and the implementation of supportive financial incentives, such as feed-in tariffs, have lowered barriers to entry for individuals, businesses, and communities, enabling them to actively participate in energy production and consumption.

One of the most significant economic drivers for the rise of prosumers is the dramatic reduction in the cost of renewable energy technologies over the past few decades. Solar PV systems, for example, have become increasingly affordable due to advancements in manufacturing processes, improvements in efficiency, and economies of scale. The average cost of solar panels has declined by more than 80% since the early 2000s, making them a cost-effective solution for households and businesses seeking to generate their own energy. Similarly, the cost of wind turbines has decreased as manufacturers have optimized designs and increased production capacities. These cost reductions have not only incentivized renewable energy adoption but also improved the financial feasibility of small-scale energy projects, enabling prosumers to realize long-term cost savings.

Battery storage systems have also seen significant cost reductions, further supporting prosumer participation. As renewable energy technologies like solar and wind are inherently intermittent, energy storage solutions are essential for balancing supply and demand. Advances in lithium-ion battery production, driven by the electric vehicle industry, have led to substantial price declines, making storage systems more accessible. Affordable battery storage allows prosumers to store excess energy generated during peak production periods and use it when needed, reducing their reliance on the grid and maximizing their return on investment.

In addition to technological cost reductions, financial incentives have played a crucial role in encouraging the adoption of renewable energy systems. Feed-in tariffs (FITs) have been one of the most effective policy mechanisms in promoting prosumer engagement. FITs provide guaranteed payments to renewable energy producers for the electricity they generate and feed into the grid. By offering long-term price certainty and stable returns, FITs have incentivized individuals, businesses, and communities to invest in renewable energy technologies. These tariffs have been particularly effective in accelerating solar and wind adoption in regions where they have been implemented, enabling prosumers to offset installation costs and generate ongoing income.

Net metering policies are another financial mechanism that has supported the rise of prosumers. Under net metering arrangements, prosumers receive credits for the excess electricity they export to the grid, which can be used to offset future energy bills. This approach reduces the financial risk associated with investing in renewable energy systems, as prosumers can directly benefit from the energy they generate. Net metering also encourages efficient energy use by aligning financial incentives with production and consumption patterns.

Government subsidies and tax credits have further lowered the upfront costs of renewable energy installations, making them more accessible to a broader range of participants. Many countries and regions offer rebates or grants to offset the cost of purchasing and installing solar panels, wind turbines, or energy storage systems. Tax incentives, such as investment tax credits for renewable energy systems, have provided additional financial relief, encouraging adoption by reducing the financial burden on prosumers.

Innovative financing models have also emerged to support the growth of energy prosumers. Third-party ownership models, such as solar leasing and power purchase agreements (PPAs), allow households and businesses to adopt renewable energy systems without significant upfront costs. Under these arrangements, a third-party company owns and maintains the renewable energy system, while the prosumer pays a monthly fee or a reduced energy rate for the electricity generated. These models make renewable energy accessible to those who may lack the financial resources for outright system ownership.

Community energy projects represent another economic driver for prosumer engagement. By pooling resources, community members can collectively invest in larger renewable energy installations, such as solar farms or wind turbines. This collaborative approach reduces individual financial barriers and allows participants to share the benefits of renewable energy generation. Community energy projects also promote social cohesion and energy equity, enabling underserved communities to access clean energy.

Chapter 2: Technologies Empowering Prosumers

The rise of energy prosumers has been driven by rapid advancements in renewable energy and digital technologies. This chapter explores the key technologies that empower individuals, businesses, and communities to generate, store, and manage their energy efficiently. From the affordability and accessibility of solar panels and wind turbines to the critical role of battery storage in addressing intermittency challenges, these innovations have transformed the energy landscape. Additionally, the development of smart grids and digital platforms, supported by the IoT, has enabled prosumers to optimize energy use and actively participate in energy markets. Together, these technologies form the backbone of the prosumer movement, providing the tools needed to decentralize energy systems and create a more sustainable and resilient future.

2.1. Renewable Energy Technologies

Renewable energy technologies are at the core of the energy prosumer movement, enabling individuals and communities to actively generate their own electricity. Among these technologies, solar PVs and small-scale wind turbines are the most widely adopted, while emerging renewable solutions offer new opportunities for diverse energy applications.

Solar PV systems have become a cornerstone of renewable energy generation for prosumers due to their affordability, scalability, and ease of installation. These systems convert sunlight directly into electricity using semiconductor materials, allowing households, businesses, and communities to harness clean energy. The declining cost of solar panels over the past two decades, driven by advancements in manufacturing and economies of scale, has made solar PV accessible to a broader audience. Additionally, their modular nature allows for flexibility in installation, from small rooftop systems for individual homes to larger arrays for community projects. Solar energy generation peaks during daylight hours, making it particularly effective for locations with consistent sunlight.

Small-scale wind turbines complement solar PV systems by providing renewable energy during periods of lower sunlight. Designed for individual or community use, these turbines generate electricity from wind power, converting kinetic energy into usable electrical energy. Small wind turbines are ideal for rural or coastal areas with steady wind patterns and can be installed on properties or shared within energy communities. While less common than solar PV systems, small-scale wind turbines play a vital role in diversifying renewable energy sources and ensuring consistent energy generation in varying weather conditions.

In addition to these well-established technologies, emerging renewable energy solutions are expanding the possibilities for prosumers. One such technology is small-scale hydropower, which generates electricity by harnessing the kinetic energy of flowing water in rivers or streams. Unlike large hydropower dams, small-scale systems are less disruptive to ecosystems and can be implemented in remote or off-grid locations. These systems are particularly beneficial for communities near water sources, offering a reliable and renewable energy option.

Another promising innovation is geothermal heat pumps, which provide both heating and cooling by utilizing the stable temperature of the Earth. These systems are highly efficient and environmentally friendly, making them an attractive option for prosumers seeking to reduce reliance on traditional heating and cooling methods. Geothermal systems can be installed on residential or commercial properties, offering long-term cost savings and energy independence.

Biomass technologies also present opportunities for renewable energy generation at the individual or community level. By converting organic materials such as agricultural waste or wood pellets into energy, biomass systems provide a sustainable energy source that can be used for heating or electricity. These systems are particularly useful in rural areas with access to biomass resources, offering a renewable alternative to fossil fuels.

2.2. Energy Storage Solutions

Energy storage solutions are essential for the effective integration of renewable energy systems into prosumer-driven energy networks. Advances in battery storage technologies have significantly improved the ability to store surplus energy generated by renewable sources such as solar and wind, ensuring energy availability when production is low. This section explores the technological progress in battery storage and its integration with renewable energy systems, highlighting its role in enabling prosumer participation and enhancing energy system resilience.

Battery storage technologies have evolved rapidly, with lithium-ion batteries emerging as the most widely used solution for both residential and commercial applications. Their high energy density, efficiency, and declining costs have made them an ideal choice for prosumers. Over the past decade, the cost of lithium-ion batteries has dropped by over 80%, driven by advancements in production and growing demand from the electric vehicle industry. This affordability has made energy storage accessible to households and businesses, allowing prosumers to store excess energy generated during peak production periods and use it during times of high demand or when renewable energy generation is unavailable.

In addition to lithium-ion batteries, other storage technologies are gaining traction, offering new opportunities for energy prosumers. Solid-state batteries, for example, promise higher energy density, longer lifespan, and improved safety compared to traditional lithium-ion systems. Similarly, flow batteries, which store energy in liquid electrolytes, provide scalability and durability, making them suitable for larger-scale applications such as community energy projects. These advancements are expanding the range of options available to prosumers, enabling them to tailor storage solutions to their specific needs.

The integration of energy storage with renewable energy systems is critical for maximizing the efficiency and reliability of prosumer energy networks. By pairing solar panels or wind turbines with battery storage, prosumers can balance the intermittency of renewable energy generation. For instance, solar panels produce energy during the day, often exceeding immediate consumption needs. Battery storage systems capture this surplus energy, allowing it to be used at night or during cloudy weather. Similarly, wind turbines may generate excess electricity during periods of high wind, which can be stored for use during calmer conditions. This integration not only enhances self-sufficiency but also reduces reliance on the grid, lowering energy costs for prosumers.

Energy storage systems also enable prosumers to participate in grid services, contributing to overall energy system stability. By discharging stored energy during peak demand periods, prosumers can help reduce strain on the grid and prevent outages. Some advanced systems even allow prosumers to engage in demand response programs, where they are compensated for adjusting energy usage based on grid conditions. This interaction between prosumers and the grid creates opportunities for economic benefits while supporting the transition to a more decentralized energy system.

2.3. Digital Tools and Platforms

Digital tools and platforms are revolutionizing the energy sector by enabling prosumers to optimize their energy use, trade surplus energy, and actively participate in decentralized energy systems. Among these innovations, blockchain technology and energy management apps play pivotal roles in empowering prosumers. Blockchain facilitates peer-to-peer (P2P) energy trading, creating transparent and secure marketplaces, while energy management apps and platforms enable efficient monitoring and control of energy production and consumption. Together, these digital advancements are reshaping the way energy is generated, shared, and consumed.

Blockchain technology has emerged as a critical enabler for P2P energy trading, allowing prosumers to directly sell their surplus energy to neighbors or local markets without relying on intermediaries. At its core, blockchain is a decentralized and secure digital ledger that records transactions in a transparent and tamper-proof manner. In the context of energy, blockchain simplifies the process of verifying energy transactions, ensuring that all parties can trust the data. This eliminates the need for traditional energy suppliers, reducing transaction costs and enabling prosumers to receive fair compensation for their energy. By decentralizing energy markets, blockchain promotes competition and innovation while fostering the growth of renewable energy systems.

One of the primary advantages of blockchain in energy trading is its ability to automate transactions through smart contracts. These self-executing contracts are coded with predefined rules, allowing energy to be traded automatically when certain conditions are met. For example, a smart contract can ensure that a prosumer's surplus solar energy is sold to a neighbor at a specified price whenever production exceeds a set threshold. This reduces the complexity of energy trading and provides a seamless experience for participants. Moreover, blockchain ensures real-time transparency by securely recording energy transactions, enabling prosumers to track their energy generation, usage, and trading activity with confidence.

Energy management apps and platforms further enhance prosumer engagement by providing tools to monitor, analyze, and control energy systems. These digital solutions integrate with renewable energy technologies, smart meters, and storage systems to deliver real-time insights into energy performance. For example, energy management apps allow prosumers to track electricity production from solar panels, monitor battery storage levels, and analyze consumption patterns. By presenting this information in user-friendly formats, these tools empower prosumers to make informed decisions about energy use, improving efficiency and reducing costs.

In addition to monitoring, energy management platforms enable automation and optimization. Advanced algorithms analyze data from various sources, such as weather forecasts and electricity prices, to recommend or implement energy-saving actions. For instance, an app might suggest running high-energy appliances during periods of peak solar generation or charging a battery when electricity prices are low. This level of automation not only maximizes the value of renewable energy systems but also aligns prosumer behavior with grid conditions, supporting overall system stability.

Some platforms also facilitate participation in demand response programs, where prosumers are incentivized to adjust their energy use based on grid needs. For example, during periods of high demand, an app might reduce consumption by temporarily lowering the energy supplied to non-essential devices. Prosumers can earn financial rewards for their participation, creating a mutually beneficial relationship between individuals and the broader energy system.

Digital tools also play a role in creating virtual energy communities, where prosumers can collaborate to share resources and benefits. These platforms connect multiple energy producers and consumers within a localized network, enabling collective energy management and P2P trading. For example, a prosumer with surplus solar energy can sell or donate it to another member of the community who needs it, fostering energy equity and strengthening local energy resilience. Blockchain technology often underpins these virtual communities, ensuring secure and transparent transactions.

Moreover, digital platforms are expanding the accessibility of renewable energy systems through innovative business models. Some platforms enable crowdfunding for renewable energy projects, allowing individuals to invest in solar or wind installations collectively. In return, participants receive a share of the energy produced or financial returns, democratizing access to renewable energy and promoting community-driven solutions.

2.4. Smart Grids and Microgrids

Smart grids and microgrids represent transformative innovations in modern energy systems, enabling more efficient, resilient, and decentralized energy management. These technologies are foundational to the rise of energy prosumers, providing the infrastructure necessary for integrating renewable energy and empowering localized energy generation. This section defines smart grids and microgrids, explains their functionalities, and highlights the benefits they bring to prosumers within decentralized energy systems.

A smart grid is an advanced energy infrastructure that uses digital technology to monitor, communicate, and manage the flow of electricity in real time. Unlike traditional grids, which rely on one-way energy distribution from centralized power plants to consumers, smart grids enable two-way communication between energy producers and consumers. This bidirectional flow allows for greater integration of renewable energy sources, real-time energy monitoring, and adaptive system management. Key components of a smart grid include smart meters, sensors, advanced communication networks, and energy management software. These elements work together to optimize energy generation, transmission, and consumption, ensuring a more efficient and reliable energy system.

Microgrids, on the other hand, are localized energy systems that can operate independently or in coordination with the main grid. A microgrid typically consists of small-scale energy generation sources, such as solar panels or wind turbines, energy storage systems, and a control system that manages energy flow. Microgrids are designed to serve specific areas, such as neighborhoods, campuses, or industrial parks, providing tailored energy solutions that address local needs. One of the defining features of a microgrid is its ability to disconnect from the main grid and operate autonomously during outages or disruptions, enhancing energy security and resilience.

The integration of smart grids and microgrids offers significant benefits to prosumers in decentralized energy systems. One major advantage is the ability to optimize energy use through real-time data and automation. Smart grids enable prosumers to monitor their energy production and consumption in detail, allowing them to identify inefficiencies and adjust their behavior accordingly. For example, a prosumer with solar panels can use smart grid data to determine the best times to run energy-intensive appliances, maximizing self-consumption and reducing reliance on the grid.

Smart grids also facilitate the seamless integration of renewable energy into the energy system. Prosumers generating solar or wind power can feed their surplus energy into the grid, contributing to the overall energy supply. Advanced grid technologies, such as automated voltage regulation and demand-response systems, ensure that this integration occurs smoothly, minimizing disruptions caused by variable energy generation. This functionality is particularly important for maintaining grid stability as renewable energy adoption increases.

Microgrids offer additional benefits by creating localized energy networks that enhance resilience and energy independence. In the event of a power outage, a microgrid can disconnect from the main grid and continue supplying electricity to its users. This capability is especially valuable for prosumers in regions prone to natural disasters or grid disruptions. By relying on local energy generation and storage, microgrids reduce dependence on centralized infrastructure, empowering communities to take control of their energy needs.

Both smart grids and microgrids support economic opportunities for prosumers by enabling P2P energy trading and participation in demand-response programs. Through smart grid platforms, prosumers can sell their surplus energy directly to neighbors or local businesses, bypassing traditional energy suppliers. This not only provides financial benefits but also fosters a sense of community and collaboration. Similarly, microgrids allow participants to share resources, optimizing energy use within the network and creating cost-saving opportunities for all members.

In addition to these benefits, smart grids and microgrids contribute to sustainability by promoting efficient energy use and reducing greenhouse gas emissions. Smart grid technologies enable load balancing, ensuring that energy demand is met with the most efficient and environmentally friendly sources available. Microgrids, with their focus on local renewable energy generation, further reduce reliance on fossil fuels, aligning with global climate goals.

Chapter 3: Policy and Regulatory Frameworks for Prosumers

The rapid growth of energy prosumers has been significantly influenced by supportive policy and regulatory frameworks. These frameworks create an enabling environment for individuals, businesses, and communities to participate in energy generation and management. This chapter examines the critical role of policy in promoting prosumer engagement, the regulatory challenges they face, and innovative approaches that support decentralized energy systems. By exploring global trends and identifying key barriers, this chapter highlights how well-designed policies and regulations can accelerate the adoption of prosumer-driven energy models, fostering a more sustainable and inclusive energy future.

3.1. Role of Policy in Promoting Prosumption

Supportive policies are crucial in enabling the widespread adoption of prosumer-driven energy systems. These policies create the framework for individuals, businesses, and communities to generate, consume, and share renewable energy, reducing reliance on centralized power plants and supporting the transition toward decentralized, sustainable energy systems. In many regions, government policies have acted as catalysts for the growth of renewable energy and prosumer participation, shaping market dynamics and encouraging innovation. Without these enabling policies, the adoption of prosumer energy models would be much slower, and the potential for achieving sustainability goals would be significantly hindered.

One of the key roles of policy in promoting prosumption is to provide financial incentives that make renewable energy technologies more affordable for consumers. Policies such as FITs, tax credits, and subsidies lower the initial financial barrier for households and businesses seeking to invest in renewable energy systems, such as solar panels and wind turbines. These incentives can guarantee a stable and predictable return on investment, helping to offset the upfront costs and making the transition to renewable energy more financially viable. By supporting prosumers financially, governments encourage greater participation in renewable energy markets, driving demand and accelerating the shift to more sustainable energy sources.

In addition to direct financial incentives, policies that address grid access and integration are also essential for promoting prosumer participation. Net metering, for example, allows prosumers to sell excess energy generated from renewable sources back to the grid, providing an economic incentive for those who produce more energy than they consume. This system helps to balance supply and demand in the grid, encourages efficient energy use, and reduces the reliance on fossil fuels. Policies that simplify the process of connecting renewable energy systems to the grid and ensure fair compensation for energy produced can significantly increase the number of prosumers.

Moreover, policies that support the development of smart grids and other digital infrastructure are key enablers of prosumer engagement. Smart grids allow for real-time monitoring and communication between energy producers and consumers, creating a more efficient and responsive energy system. By incorporating renewable energy sources into a smart grid, prosumers can manage their energy production and consumption more effectively. Policies that incentivize the development of these technologies help to lower the cost of integration and ensure that energy systems are adaptable to the growing role of prosumers.

Another critical policy area is the regulation of energy markets. In many countries, energy markets are structured around large utility companies, which can create barriers to entry for smaller, decentralized energy producers. Policy frameworks that encourage competition, such as those that allow for P2P energy trading or community-based energy initiatives, can provide prosumers with the opportunity to trade energy directly with one another, bypassing traditional utility companies. This decentralized approach creates more opportunities for prosumers to profit from their renewable energy generation and allows for more equitable energy access, especially in underserved communities.

Finally, policies that promote education and awareness about the benefits of prosumption are essential for ensuring that the broader population understands and embraces the shift toward renewable energy. Public awareness campaigns, incentives for energy-efficient technologies, and programs to educate consumers about energy management can increase participation in prosumer models. As more individuals and communities understand the economic, environmental, and social benefits of renewable energy, the adoption of prosumption is likely to grow.

3.2. Regulatory Challenges

As energy prosumers become more prevalent, integrating them into existing energy systems presents significant regulatory challenges. Traditional energy infrastructure and market structures were designed around centralized power generation, with large utility companies controlling the production, distribution, and consumption of electricity. The rise of decentralized prosumer-driven energy models, while offering numerous benefits, requires substantial changes to existing regulations to ensure efficient and equitable integration. The challenges in this process include barriers related to grid access, regulatory frameworks, and concerns about equity and access for all potential prosumers.

One of the main barriers to integrating prosumers into existing energy systems is the incompatibility between decentralized energy production and traditional grid infrastructure. Most energy grids were not designed to handle the two-way flow of electricity that prosumers generate and feed back into the system. In many cases, traditional grids are structured to distribute power from a central point to consumers, not to accommodate the input of energy from numerous small-scale, decentralized sources. Upgrading grid infrastructure to allow for seamless integration of renewable energy from prosumers requires significant investment in smart grid technologies, which can manage real-time energy flows, monitor energy consumption, and ensure that the grid remains stable despite fluctuations in renewable energy production.

In addition to infrastructure challenges, regulatory frameworks often fail to support the full integration of prosumers. Many regions still operate under outdated regulatory models that focus on utility-scale generation and neglect the growing role of decentralized energy producers. As a result, prosumers often face difficulties accessing the grid or receiving fair compensation for the energy they produce. For instance, grid access fees or discriminatory pricing structures can discourage individuals and communities from investing in renewable energy systems. In some cases, the lack of clear and consistent rules regarding energy trading and compensation can create confusion and uncertainty, further inhibiting prosumer participation.

Another regulatory challenge involves the lack of policies to support P2P energy trading. In decentralized systems, prosumers may want to exchange energy directly with one another, bypassing traditional utility companies. However, legal and regulatory barriers, such as licensing requirements and market rules, often prevent P2P trading from becoming a widespread practice. In some jurisdictions, the energy market is highly regulated, with utilities holding exclusive rights to the distribution and sale of electricity. Allowing P2P trading would require significant changes to energy market regulations, including the establishment of clear frameworks for transactions, pricing, and grid integration.

Equity and access are also key concerns when it comes to integrating prosumers into existing energy systems. While prosumer participation in renewable energy generation can provide economic and environmental benefits, these advantages are not always accessible to everyone. The high upfront costs of renewable energy systems, such as solar panels or wind turbines, can be prohibitive for low-income households or those in underserved communities. In many cases, individuals and communities without the necessary financial resources or access to capital cannot afford to invest in renewable energy technologies, limiting the potential for broad prosumer participation.

Moreover, there are concerns about the potential for increased inequality in the energy sector if policies do not specifically address energy access for marginalized groups. If renewable energy systems are predominantly adopted by wealthier households or communities, the benefits of decentralized energy production may not be shared equitably, leaving low-income households reliant on centralized, fossil fuel-based energy sources. Without targeted policies to promote equitable access to renewable energy technologies, the gap between those who can afford to participate in prosumption and those who cannot may widen, exacerbating existing inequalities in energy access.

3.3. Innovative Policy Approaches

As the energy landscape shifts toward decentralized, renewable energy systems, innovative policy approaches are essential to fostering prosumer participation and ensuring that energy markets are inclusive, efficient, and sustainable. Policies such as dynamic pricing models, net metering, and community energy schemes have emerged as effective tools for integrating prosumers into existing energy systems. These approaches not only incentivize the adoption of renewable energy technologies but also promote equitable access to energy and encourage collaboration among communities. This section explores these innovative policy frameworks and their role in advancing prosumption.

Dynamic pricing models are a significant innovation in energy policy that allows for more flexible and efficient pricing based on real-time supply and demand conditions. Unlike traditional flat-rate pricing, which charges consumers a fixed amount regardless of when or how much energy they use, dynamic pricing adjusts electricity prices to reflect fluctuations in energy demand and availability. For instance, during periods of low demand or high renewable energy generation, prices may decrease, encouraging prosumers to consume energy or charge their storage systems when it is abundant and inexpensive. Conversely, during periods of high demand or low renewable generation, prices may rise, signaling to prosumers to reduce consumption or contribute stored energy back to the grid.

Dynamic pricing models benefit prosumers by offering the potential for cost savings and encouraging more efficient energy use. By providing incentives to use or store energy during off-peak times, these models help to reduce pressure on the grid and promote a more stable energy system. Additionally, dynamic pricing aligns the interests of prosumers with those of the broader energy system, creating a more responsive and resilient network. As more prosumers generate and store renewable energy, dynamic pricing ensures that their participation is financially rewarding, further incentivizing renewable energy adoption.

Net metering policies are another innovative approach that has played a critical role in promoting prosumer engagement. Net metering allows prosumers who generate renewable energy to feed surplus electricity back into the grid in exchange for credits or payments. These credits can then be used to offset energy consumption during times when production is lower, such as at night or on cloudy days. Essentially, net metering provides a financial incentive for prosumers to install renewable energy systems by allowing them to "store" their excess energy in the grid and "draw" from it when needed, creating a more balanced and flexible energy system.

Net metering policies vary by region, but they have been particularly effective in encouraging solar energy adoption. By offering a fair compensation mechanism, net metering makes renewable energy systems more financially viable for prosumers, particularly those in areas with high energy costs. This policy approach not only helps to reduce the financial burden of renewable energy investments but also fosters a more equitable energy system by enabling prosumers to share their excess generation with the wider community. Additionally, net metering contributes to grid stability by ensuring that surplus energy from prosumers is absorbed and distributed where it is needed most.

Community energy schemes and collective ownership models represent another innovative policy approach that encourages collaboration and shared benefits among prosumers. These models allow individuals or communities to collectively invest in renewable energy projects, such as solar farms, wind turbines, or biomass facilities, and share the generated energy or profits. In community energy schemes, participants may purchase shares in a project and receive dividends from the energy produced, or they may receive energy credits to offset their own consumption. Collective ownership models are particularly beneficial for individuals or groups who may not have the financial resources or suitable land to invest in renewable energy systems independently.

Community energy projects offer several advantages, including economies of scale, lower costs for participants, and increased social cohesion. By pooling resources, community members can invest in larger renewable energy systems that may be more efficient and cost-effective than individual installations. These projects can also provide a platform for community engagement and empowerment, allowing local residents to take control of their energy production and consumption. Community energy schemes also help to democratize energy access, ensuring that renewable energy benefits are shared more equitably across communities.

In addition to fostering collaboration within communities, collective ownership models can also contribute to energy justice by providing access to renewable energy for underserved or low-income populations. By lowering the financial barriers to renewable energy participation, these models enable marginalized groups to benefit from clean, affordable energy. Furthermore, community energy projects can support local economic development by creating jobs and generating revenue that stays within the community, rather than flowing to large utility companies or external investors.

3.4. Global Trends in Prosumer Policies

As the role of energy prosumers grows worldwide, various countries and regions have developed innovative regulatory frameworks to encourage participation and integration of decentralized renewable energy systems. These forward-thinking policies not only support the adoption of renewable energy technologies but also create more resilient, sustainable, and equitable energy systems. This section examines examples of pioneering regulatory frameworks from around the globe and the lessons learned from these regions in fostering prosumer participation.

One of the most notable examples of progressive prosumer policies is found in Germany, where the Energiewende, or energy transition, has been a central component of the country's energy policy since the early 2000s. Germany's policies have focused on the promotion of renewable energy, energy efficiency, and the decentralization of energy systems. The Renewable Energy Sources Act (EEG), introduced in 2000, established one of the first feed-in tariff (FIT) systems to encourage the adoption of renewable energy. Under the EEG, prosumers are guaranteed fixed payments for the renewable energy they produce and feed into the grid. This policy has played a pivotal role in Germany becoming one of the world leaders in solar and wind energy deployment.

Over time, Germany has adjusted its prosumer policies to reflect the evolving energy landscape. For example, the country's Energiewende also includes provisions for self-consumption of renewable energy, allowing prosumers to use the energy they produce without being taxed on it, incentivizing the installation of residential solar systems. Additionally, Germany has supported the development of smart grids to better integrate renewable energy into the broader energy system. As the energy sector has become more decentralized, the government has focused on improving grid flexibility, making it easier for prosumers to sell their excess energy back into the system.

Germany's experience demonstrates the importance of long-term, consistent policy support in creating a stable market for renewable energy prosumers. The country's early investments in FITs and grid infrastructure have provided a strong foundation for prosumer engagement, though ongoing adjustments have been necessary to keep pace with rapidly advancing technology and the growth of decentralized energy production. The main lesson from Germany's experience is the importance of designing policies that evolve with the market, adapting to changing technological, economic, and environmental circumstances.

Another notable example comes from the United States, where states like California and Hawaii have been pioneers in implementing prosumer-friendly policies. California's Net Energy Metering (NEM) program, which allows prosumers to receive credits for the excess solar energy they generate, has played a significant role in increasing solar energy adoption across the state. The state has also implemented time-of-use (TOU) pricing, which charges higher rates during peak energy demand times and lower rates during off-peak hours. This dynamic pricing model incentivizes prosumers to produce and store energy when it is most beneficial to the grid.

California has also integrated advanced smart grid technologies, which enhance the management of distributed energy resources (DERs). This integration allows for better coordination between energy producers and consumers, enabling the grid to be more responsive and efficient. Additionally, California has been exploring VPPs, where groups of distributed energy resources are aggregated to provide grid services, demonstrating how prosumers can contribute to grid stability in real-time. These innovations highlight the role of smart technologies and dynamic pricing in supporting the participation of prosumers in the energy system.

In Hawaii, the transition to renewable energy has been driven by policies that support both self-consumption and grid integration of renewable energy. Hawaii's Grid Modernization Strategy aims to improve the state's grid infrastructure to accommodate higher levels of renewable energy, particularly from distributed sources like rooftop solar. Hawaii has also implemented demand response programs, where prosumers are rewarded for reducing their energy consumption during peak demand periods. These initiatives not only support renewable energy adoption but also improve the overall efficiency and resilience of the grid, particularly in remote or isolated areas where energy supply may be limited.

Both California and Hawaii's policies underscore the importance of providing incentives for both energy production and consumption, as well as the integration of advanced grid technologies. The lessons learned from these regions emphasize the need for a comprehensive approach to prosumer policies, combining financial incentives, dynamic pricing, grid modernization, and innovative market structures to maximize the participation of decentralized energy producers.

In the United Kingdom, Ofgem (the Office of Gas and Electricity Markets) has been working on initiatives to make the energy system more flexible and inclusive for prosumers. The UK has focused on reducing regulatory barriers that prevent prosumers from accessing the energy market, particularly by simplifying the process of connecting to the grid. The government has also explored models for community energy schemes, which allow local groups to jointly invest in and benefit from renewable energy projects. These schemes help ensure that the benefits of prosumption are distributed more equitably, fostering energy democracy and empowering communities to take control of their energy future.

The UK's efforts to streamline regulatory processes and promote community energy demonstrate the importance of ensuring that prosumer policies are accessible and inclusive. Reducing barriers to entry and supporting community-based projects can facilitate wider participation and create more localized benefits, particularly for marginalized or underserved populations.

Chapter 4: Economic and Social Impacts of Prosumers

The rise of energy prosumers extends beyond technological and environmental benefits, with significant economic and social implications for individuals, communities, and society at large. This chapter explores the economic advantages of prosumer participation, such as cost savings, job creation, and market innovation, while also addressing the challenges related to energy equity and access. Additionally, it examines the social effects of prosumer engagement, from fostering community resilience and collaboration to driving broader social change. By understanding these economic and social impacts, we can better appreciate the role prosumers play in creating a more sustainable, inclusive, and equitable energy system.

4.1. Economic Benefits

The rise of energy prosumers offers a range of significant economic benefits for households, businesses, and society at large. By generating their own renewable energy, prosumers can reduce their reliance on conventional electricity from the grid, leading to substantial cost savings. Additionally, the growth of prosumer-driven energy systems has spurred job creation in renewable energy technologies, energy management, and related sectors, providing economic opportunities in both local and global contexts.

For households, one of the primary economic benefits of becoming a prosumer is the reduction in energy costs. With the installation of renewable energy systems such as solar panels or small-scale wind turbines, households can generate their own electricity, significantly lowering their utility bills. This is particularly advantageous in regions with high electricity prices or areas where grid infrastructure is less reliable. Through the use of energy storage solutions, such as batteries, households can store excess energy generated during periods of high production (e.g., during the day for solar power) and use it during times of high demand or low generation, further enhancing their ability to reduce reliance on the grid.

In addition to energy cost savings, prosumers can also benefit financially by participating in programs like net metering or feed-in tariffs. These programs allow prosumers to sell excess energy back to the grid or receive credits for the electricity they generate. By taking advantage of these schemes, prosumers can recover their initial investment in renewable energy systems more quickly and even generate ongoing income from their energy production. The combination of cost savings and financial incentives makes renewable energy systems an increasingly attractive investment for households, leading to long-term economic benefits.

For businesses, the adoption of renewable energy technologies offers similar advantages. By investing in on-site renewable energy generation, such as solar panels or wind turbines, companies can reduce operational costs by lowering their energy bills. This is especially beneficial for energy-intensive industries, where electricity costs can be a significant portion of overall expenses. Renewable energy systems also provide businesses with greater energy security and resilience, especially in regions prone to power outages or grid instability. By producing their own energy, businesses can ensure a more reliable and consistent power supply, reducing the risk of disruptions to their operations.

In addition to cost savings, the shift toward prosumer energy systems has also created significant job opportunities in the renewable energy and technology sectors. The demand for solar panels, wind turbines, battery storage solutions, and smart grid technologies has led to the growth of a global renewable energy industry, generating jobs across a wide range of fields. These include manufacturing, installation, maintenance, and energy management. As more households and businesses adopt renewable energy technologies, the need for skilled workers in these areas continues to rise, creating local employment opportunities and boosting regional economies.

The renewable energy sector has also spurred innovation, leading to the development of new technologies and business models. The growth of smart grid infrastructure, which enables two-way communication between energy producers and consumers, has created jobs in the tech and software development industries. The expansion of P2P energy trading platforms and VPPs has further fueled the demand for new software and digital solutions that allow prosumers to trade energy, manage consumption, and optimize energy storage.

4.2. Challenges in Energy Equity

While the rise of energy prosumers brings significant benefits, it also presents challenges related to energy equity. As more individuals and communities adopt renewable energy technologies, disparities in access to these technologies can create or exacerbate existing inequalities. Addressing these challenges is essential to ensure that the benefits of prosumption are shared widely and that all individuals, regardless of socio-economic status or geographic location, can participate in the transition to a more sustainable and decentralized energy system.

One of the primary barriers to prosumer adoption is the high initial cost of renewable energy technologies, such as solar panels, wind turbines, and energy storage systems. Although the costs of these technologies have decreased significantly over the past decade, they can still be prohibitively expensive for low-income households or communities without access to capital. The upfront costs of purchasing and installing renewable energy systems, coupled with the cost of any necessary infrastructure upgrades (such as grid connections), can prevent many individuals from accessing the benefits of prosumption. Without financial support, incentives, or subsidies, households in lower-income brackets may be unable to invest in renewable energy solutions, leaving them reliant on traditional, often more expensive, energy sources.

In addition to financial barriers, disparities in access to prosumer technologies can also be influenced by geographic location. Rural and remote communities, for example, may face unique challenges in adopting renewable energy technologies. These communities may lack the infrastructure necessary to connect to the grid or may be situated in areas with insufficient sunlight or wind resources for effective energy generation. Additionally, the availability of qualified technicians and installers may be limited in these areas, making it more difficult for residents to install, maintain, or repair renewable energy systems. As a result, rural and underserved communities may be left behind in the transition to decentralized, renewable energy systems, further deepening energy inequality.

Another challenge in achieving energy equity is the concentration of renewable energy adoption in wealthier neighborhoods or areas with higher property values. Those with more financial resources are more likely to be able to afford the upfront costs of renewable energy systems and may also benefit from incentives such as tax credits, grants, or subsidies. Conversely, lower-income households may struggle to access these benefits due to financial constraints, leaving wealthier individuals and businesses to reap the economic and environmental advantages of renewable energy. As a result, the unequal distribution of prosumer technologies can exacerbate existing disparities in energy access, creating a divide between those who can afford renewable energy and those who cannot.

The potential risks of leaving underserved communities behind are significant. If energy prosumption is largely confined to wealthier households and businesses, the broader societal benefits of decentralized energy systems, such as reduced greenhouse gas emissions and energy independence, may not be fully realized. Furthermore, the economic benefits of prosumer participation, including cost savings and the opportunity to sell surplus energy, may be restricted to a small segment of the population. This could perpetuate energy poverty and social inequality, undermining efforts to create a more inclusive and sustainable energy system.

To address these challenges, policymakers must prioritize the inclusion of underserved communities in the prosumer transition. This includes providing targeted financial support and incentives for low-income households to invest in renewable energy systems, as well as expanding access to energy storage and smart grid technologies. Policies should also focus on reducing geographic disparities by supporting infrastructure development in rural and remote areas and ensuring that technicians and installers are available to meet the needs of these communities. Additionally, promoting community energy projects, where groups of individuals or businesses can collectively invest in renewable energy infrastructure, can help to democratize access and reduce the barriers to entry for those who may not be able to afford individual systems.

4.3. Social Implications

The rise of energy prosumers is not only reshaping the way energy is produced and consumed but also has significant social implications that extend beyond the energy sector. By actively participating in energy generation, prosumers are becoming agents of societal change, driving progress toward more sustainable, equitable, and resilient communities. Through the adoption of renewable energy technologies and the creation of shared energy projects, prosumers are fostering stronger community bonds, empowering local economies, and contributing to the broader goal of environmental sustainability.

Prosumers, through their engagement in decentralized energy systems, are playing a transformative role in shifting societal attitudes towards energy. Traditionally, energy consumers have been passive participants in the energy market, relying on centralized utilities for their energy needs. Prosumers, on the other hand, take on the dual role of both producers and consumers, actively managing their energy production, consumption, and storage. This shift in behavior fosters a sense of ownership and responsibility for energy resources, encouraging individuals and communities to become more mindful of their energy use and environmental impact.

As agents of change, prosumers contribute to a cultural shift that values sustainability and environmental stewardship. By investing in renewable energy systems, such as solar panels and wind turbines, prosumers are helping to reduce reliance on fossil fuels, lower greenhouse gas emissions, and mitigate the effects of climate change. This shift toward cleaner energy sources not only benefits the environment but also serves as a model for others to follow, inspiring greater collective action. As more individuals and communities embrace prosumption, the broader adoption of renewable energy becomes more normalized, creating a societal culture that prioritizes sustainability.

In addition to their role in environmental change, prosumers also play an important part in shaping social dynamics within their communities. One of the most significant social implications of prosumer engagement is the strengthening of community bonds through shared energy projects. Community energy schemes, in which groups of individuals or local organizations collectively invest in renewable energy infrastructure, foster collaboration and create opportunities for local empowerment. These projects enable participants to pool resources and share the benefits of renewable energy production, reducing individual financial barriers and increasing collective resilience.

Shared energy projects, such as community solar or wind farms, provide a platform for individuals to collaborate and contribute to a common goal. By working together, community members can invest in larger-scale renewable energy systems that might otherwise be unaffordable for any single individual. In return, participants can benefit from the energy generated, either through direct consumption or by receiving a share of the financial profits from energy sales. This sense of shared ownership helps to foster a spirit of cooperation and mutual support, strengthening community ties and enhancing local solidarity.

Beyond the tangible benefits of shared energy production, these projects also contribute to social cohesion by addressing local energy needs and providing a sense of empowerment. Communities that participate in energy generation can experience increased energy independence, reducing their reliance on external energy suppliers and protecting themselves from price fluctuations and supply disruptions. This empowerment fosters a greater sense of control over one's energy future, reinforcing the social bonds that make communities more resilient and self-sufficient.

Moreover, the development of shared energy projects can have positive economic and social impacts on local economies. By investing in renewable energy infrastructure, communities can create jobs, stimulate local economic growth, and foster innovation. These projects often require skilled labor for installation, maintenance, and management, providing employment opportunities for local workers. Additionally, the revenues generated from energy sales can be reinvested into community development projects, further enhancing local well-being and promoting social and economic sustainability.

The adoption of prosumer-driven energy models also has the potential to address social equity issues by providing access to affordable, clean energy in underserved or marginalized communities. In many regions, energy costs are a significant burden for low-income households, and the lack of access to reliable, affordable energy can exacerbate existing social inequalities. Community energy projects and collective ownership models can provide these households with a more equitable path to energy access, enabling them to benefit from renewable energy while reducing their energy costs. By democratizing energy production, prosumers contribute to greater energy justice, ensuring that the benefits of renewable energy are accessible to all members of society.

4.4. Resilience and Energy Security

Energy resilience and security are central concerns in the modern energy landscape, particularly as climate change and other global challenges put pressure on existing infrastructure. Prosumers—individuals, businesses, and communities who generate, consume, and sometimes share energy—play an increasingly important role in enhancing the stability and reliability of energy systems. Through their contributions to grid stability and the promotion of energy independence, prosumers are helping to create more resilient and secure energy networks that can better withstand disruptions and reduce vulnerabilities.

One of the key ways in which prosumers contribute to grid stability is by generating renewable energy locally, reducing the strain on centralized power plants and transmission lines. Traditional energy systems rely on large, centralized power plants that generate electricity and send it to consumers through long-distance transmission lines. These systems are vulnerable to disruptions, such as power outages caused by weather events, technical failures, or accidents. In contrast, prosumers, by producing energy on-site from renewable sources such as solar, wind, or small-scale hydro, contribute to the decentralization of energy production. This distributed generation model helps to relieve pressure on the grid, particularly during peak demand times, and allows for a more flexible, responsive energy system.

The integration of prosumers into the energy grid enables greater redundancy, which enhances overall system reliability. When a centralized power plant experiences a failure or is knocked offline due to extreme weather or other factors, the distributed energy sources provided by prosumers can help fill the gap, maintaining a steady flow of electricity to the grid. Additionally, prosumers can store excess energy generated during periods of low demand (using battery storage systems or other energy storage technologies) and feed it back into the grid during peak demand periods. This process, known as "demand-side management," helps to balance energy supply and demand, contributing to overall grid stability.

Another important aspect of prosumer engagement in grid stability is the role of smart grids. Smart grids use advanced communication and control technologies to enable real-time monitoring and management of electricity flow between prosumers, utilities, and other grid operators. Through smart grid systems, prosumers can track energy production and consumption, adjust their usage based on grid conditions, and participate in demand-response programs. For example, during times of grid stress, prosumers may be incentivized to reduce their energy consumption or discharge stored energy, providing much-needed relief to the grid. These systems also allow for better integration of renewable energy sources, as they can accommodate fluctuations in energy generation caused by changing weather conditions, such as cloud cover or variable wind speeds. By enabling more efficient energy management and facilitating real-time coordination, smart grids help to enhance the stability and resilience of energy systems.

Prosumers also contribute to enhanced energy independence, an important aspect of energy security. By producing their own renewable energy, prosumers reduce their reliance on external energy suppliers and centralized grid systems, which are often subject to price fluctuations, supply disruptions, or geopolitical tensions. In regions where access to reliable energy is limited, prosumers can increase their energy security by installing off-grid renewable energy systems, such as solar panels coupled with energy storage. This autonomy provides greater control over energy access, particularly in remote or underserved areas where grid infrastructure may be insufficient or unreliable.

Energy independence can also have economic benefits for prosumers. By generating their own energy, households and businesses can lower their electricity bills and reduce their exposure to rising energy costs. In some cases, prosumers can even earn revenue by selling surplus energy back to the grid, further improving their financial stability. This increased financial resilience can be particularly important in regions where energy costs are high or fluctuate unpredictably. For businesses, energy independence can reduce operational costs, making it easier to maintain consistent operations and mitigate the financial risks associated with fluctuating energy prices.

Furthermore, prosumers play a key role in increasing energy resilience by creating more diversified and flexible energy systems. In areas that are prone to natural disasters, such as hurricanes, earthquakes, or floods, traditional energy infrastructure is often vulnerable to damage, leading to long-term power outages. By incorporating renewable energy systems at the local level, prosumers help to ensure that power can be quickly restored in the event of a disaster. For example, communities with a significant number of prosumers may be able to operate on a microgrid, allowing them to continue generating and consuming energy even if the main grid is down. These systems provide a backup energy supply and allow affected communities to maintain essential services until the broader grid is restored.

The resilience and energy security benefits of prosumers also extend to national and regional energy systems. A greater proportion of renewable energy generation by prosumers reduces the overall reliance on imported fossil fuels, helping to mitigate the risks associated with fuel supply disruptions and price volatility. Additionally, decentralized energy production can reduce the environmental impact of energy systems, contributing to national efforts to meet climate goals and reduce greenhouse gas emissions. By enhancing energy independence at the local and national levels, prosumers help to create more resilient, sustainable, and secure energy systems.

Chapter 5: The Role of Energy Communities

Energy communities are emerging as powerful drivers of the decentralized energy transition, where individuals and local groups collaborate to produce, manage, and share renewable energy. This chapter delves into the significance of energy communities in fostering collective action for sustainable energy production and consumption. It explores the key characteristics of energy communities, the various governance and management models they employ, and the benefits they bring, including economic opportunities, social cohesion, and enhanced energy resilience. Additionally, the chapter addresses the barriers to their implementation and the strategies needed to scale these models effectively. By understanding the role of energy communities, we can better appreciate how collaborative energy solutions contribute to a more inclusive and sustainable energy future.

5.1. Defining Energy Communities

Energy communities represent a collective approach to energy generation and consumption, where groups of individuals, businesses, or organizations work together to produce, share, and manage renewable energy. These communities aim to reduce reliance on centralized energy systems, lower energy costs, and promote sustainable practices. Energy communities can range from small, local initiatives to larger, more organized networks, and they play a crucial role in the transition to decentralized, renewable energy systems. This section explores the characteristics and key components of energy communities, highlighting the differences between individual and collective prosumers.

The core characteristic of an energy community is its collective nature. Rather than individual prosumers acting alone, energy communities bring together members who share a common interest in generating and managing energy locally. These communities typically focus on renewable energy sources, such as solar, wind, or biomass, and may include shared infrastructure, such as solar panels, wind turbines, or energy storage systems. By pooling resources, members of an energy community can invest in larger-scale renewable energy projects that would otherwise be unaffordable or impractical for individual prosumers. In return, participants benefit from lower energy costs, shared revenue from energy sales, and increased energy resilience.

One key component of energy communities is their governance model. Energy communities are often organized as cooperatives, non-profits, or other legal entities that enable collective decision-making and management. This governance structure ensures that all members have a voice in how energy resources are managed and how profits are distributed. Cooperative models, for example, allow members to share ownership of renewable energy systems and vote on important decisions related to the operation of the community. This democratic approach fosters a sense of ownership and accountability among participants, encouraging active engagement and long-term commitment to sustainable energy practices.

Another important aspect of energy communities is the integration of renewable energy technologies with energy storage and management systems. These systems allow members to store surplus energy for later use, optimize consumption, and manage fluctuations in energy supply. In some cases, energy communities can also participate in local or regional energy markets, selling excess energy back to the grid or engaging in P2P energy trading. By doing so, they can generate income, further reducing costs for members, and contribute to overall grid stability. The combination of shared energy generation, storage, and management systems enables energy communities to become self-sufficient, reduce energy costs, and enhance local energy security.

Energy communities differ significantly from individual prosumers, who typically generate and consume energy independently. While individual prosumers may invest in small-scale renewable energy systems, such as rooftop solar panels or home wind turbines, they do so primarily for personal use. Although individual prosumers may share excess energy with the grid, their ability to collaborate with others on a larger scale is limited. In contrast, energy communities leverage collective investment, shared resources, and collaborative decision-making to optimize energy production and consumption on a larger scale. This collective approach allows for economies of scale, greater energy efficiency, and more significant environmental and economic impacts than individual prosumer efforts.

5.2. Governance and Management Models

Energy communities are structured in various governance models, with the most common being cooperative and non-profit models. These models are designed to enable collective ownership, democratic decision-making, and the equitable distribution of benefits. They play a critical role in ensuring that energy communities are not only economically viable but also socially inclusive, fostering active participation and engagement from all members. This section explores the cooperative and non-profit governance models for energy communities, focusing on their organizational structures and their emphasis on transparent decision-making and fair distribution of resources.

The cooperative model is one of the most widely adopted governance structures for energy communities. Cooperatives are member-owned and member-controlled organizations, where each participant has an equal say in decision-making, regardless of the size of their energy contribution or investment. In an energy cooperative, members typically pool their resources to finance and operate renewable energy systems such as solar arrays or wind farms. This model promotes shared ownership and ensures that the benefits of renewable energy are distributed fairly among participants. Additionally, cooperatives often prioritize environmental and social goals over profit maximization, aligning the community's interests with broader sustainability objectives.

One of the key advantages of energy cooperatives is their democratic governance structure. Decision-making in cooperatives is usually based on the principle of "one member, one vote," meaning that every member has an equal say in the governance of the cooperative. This egalitarian approach fosters a sense of ownership and accountability, encouraging active participation in the cooperative's operations. Cooperatives typically hold annual general meetings (AGMs) where members can discuss and vote on important issues, such as investment decisions, energy management strategies, and the distribution of profits. These meetings serve as a platform for open communication, enabling members to engage with one another, share concerns, and make collective decisions that reflect the community's values and goals.

In contrast to cooperatives, non-profit organizations are another common governance model for energy communities. Non-profits are usually formed with the primary goal of serving the public interest rather than generating profit for shareholders. In the context of energy communities, non-profit organizations are typically responsible for managing renewable energy projects, such as community solar farms or wind turbines, on behalf of local residents or businesses. These organizations may work with local governments, businesses, or other stakeholders to fund and implement energy systems that benefit the broader community. The non-profit model emphasizes environmental sustainability and social equity, aiming to reduce energy costs for participants and support local economic development.

Non-profit energy communities may have a more hierarchical structure than cooperatives, with a board of directors or trustees responsible for making high-level decisions. However, many non-profit energy communities still prioritize transparency and accountability, providing opportunities for stakeholders to participate in decision-making processes. This may include regular community meetings, consultations with stakeholders, and annual reports that outline the organization's activities, financial performance, and progress toward sustainability goals.

One of the key aspects of both cooperative and non-profit energy communities is the importance of transparent decision-making.

Transparency ensures that all members or stakeholders are informed about the community's activities, financial situation, and future plans. In both governance models, open communication channels are essential to building trust among members and fostering a sense of collective responsibility. Regular updates on the status of energy projects, including financial performance and energy production, help members make informed decisions about how the community operates and whether it is meeting its sustainability and financial goals. Transparency also allows members to hold the governing body accountable for its actions, ensuring that decisions align with the community's best interests.

Equitable distribution of benefits is another fundamental principle of governance in energy communities. In both cooperative and non-profit models, the aim is to ensure that all members have access to the benefits of renewable energy, regardless of their financial resources or level of participation. The equitable distribution of benefits can take various forms, such as reducing energy costs for low-income households, providing financial incentives to members who generate surplus energy, or reinvesting profits into local community development projects. In cooperatives, the distribution of profits is often based on the amount of energy contributed or consumed, while in non-profit organizations, the benefits may be shared more broadly to address social or environmental priorities.

For energy communities to be successful in achieving social and environmental goals, the governance model must promote inclusivity and avoid reinforcing existing inequalities. This is particularly important in marginalized or low-income communities, where access to clean, affordable energy can be limited. Policies that prioritize the inclusion of diverse community members, including those who may not have the financial means to invest in energy systems, can help ensure that energy communities provide equitable benefits for all.

5.3. Benefits of Energy Communities

Energy communities provide numerous benefits, both from an economic and social perspective. By collaborating on energy generation and management, members can leverage the advantages of collective action to lower costs, improve energy efficiency, and increase the overall impact of their renewable energy projects. Additionally, energy communities foster social cohesion and local empowerment by bringing together individuals with a shared commitment to sustainability, energy independence, and community well-being. This section explores the economic benefits, such as economies of scale in energy generation and storage, as well as the social benefits, including strengthened community ties and greater local control over energy resources.

One of the primary economic benefits of energy communities is the ability to achieve economies of scale in energy generation and storage. When individual households or businesses invest in renewable energy systems, such as solar panels or wind turbines, the cost per unit of energy generated can be relatively high due to the small scale of the project. However, by pooling resources and investing collectively, energy communities can fund larger, more efficient renewable energy systems that benefit all members. For example, a community solar farm allows multiple households or businesses to share the costs and benefits of a single, large-scale solar installation. The larger system can take advantage of technological efficiencies and lower per-unit costs, making renewable energy more affordable for participants.

Economies of scale also extend to energy storage. In a collective energy storage system, the cost of installing and maintaining batteries or other storage technologies can be shared across all members, reducing the financial burden on any single participant. Energy storage is a crucial component of renewable energy systems, as it allows communities to store excess energy generated during periods of high production and use it during times of low generation. By investing in shared storage solutions, energy communities can maximize their ability to use renewable energy efficiently, reduce reliance on the grid, and lower their overall energy costs. This collaborative approach not only reduces the financial barriers to adopting renewable energy but also enhances the economic sustainability of energy communities.

Beyond the economic advantages, energy communities also offer significant social benefits. One of the most important social benefits is the strengthening of social cohesion. Energy communities bring together people who share a common interest in sustainability, renewable energy, and local empowerment. By working together to invest in and manage renewable energy systems, community members build relationships based on trust, cooperation, and shared goals. These strong social bonds foster a sense of belonging and collective responsibility, which can lead to greater participation in other community projects and initiatives.

Furthermore, energy communities provide a platform for local empowerment. In traditional, centralized energy systems, control over energy generation and distribution is typically in the hands of large utilities or corporations, leaving local communities with little influence over their energy resources. Energy communities, on the other hand, enable individuals and groups to take control of their energy production, consumption, and management. This sense of empowerment helps communities become more self-sufficient and resilient in the face of energy disruptions or price fluctuations. For example, in the event of a power outage or natural disaster, an energy community with its own renewable energy systems and storage capacity can continue to operate independently of the grid, providing energy security and peace of mind to its members.

In addition to enhancing energy security, local empowerment through energy communities also encourages broader civic engagement. Community energy projects often involve a collaborative decision-making process, where members have a say in the design, operation, and governance of the energy systems. This participatory approach fosters a greater sense of ownership and responsibility among community members, motivating them to actively contribute to the success of the project. It also ensures that the energy systems reflect the needs and priorities of the community, rather than being dictated by external interests.

Energy communities also play a crucial role in addressing social equity. By democratizing access to renewable energy and reducing the costs associated with energy generation and storage, these communities can help lower-income households and underserved populations access affordable, clean energy. In many cases, energy communities enable residents who may not have the financial means to invest in renewable energy technologies individually to benefit from collective energy projects. Additionally, community-driven projects can help bridge the gap in energy access in rural or remote areas, where traditional energy infrastructure may be lacking or unreliable.

Another key social benefit of energy communities is the potential for economic development. The establishment and operation of renewable energy projects can create jobs in the local community, including opportunities in installation, maintenance, energy management, and project development. These jobs help to stimulate the local economy, providing income and employment opportunities for community members. Furthermore, energy communities can generate revenue from the sale of surplus energy or other services, which can be reinvested in local development initiatives, such as education, healthcare, or infrastructure improvements.

5.4. Barriers to Implementation

While energy communities offer significant benefits, several barriers to their successful implementation persist. These challenges include financial, technical, and regulatory hurdles that can inhibit the widespread adoption of collective renewable energy projects. Additionally, there may be community resistance to adopting new technologies, particularly in areas where traditional energy systems are deeply ingrained or where there is limited awareness of the potential benefits of energy communities. Addressing these barriers is essential for unlocking the full potential of energy communities and ensuring their long-term success.

One of the most significant financial barriers to the implementation of energy communities is the high upfront cost of renewable energy infrastructure. Although the cost of renewable energy technologies, such as solar panels and wind turbines, has decreased significantly over the past decade, the initial capital required for large-scale projects can still be prohibitive for many communities, especially those in low-income areas. Additionally, the cost of energy storage systems, which are necessary for balancing intermittent renewable energy generation, can further increase the financial burden on community projects. Without access to affordable financing options or subsidies, many energy communities may struggle to secure the necessary funding to develop renewable energy systems.

To address these financial challenges, policymakers and financial institutions need to develop innovative financing mechanisms, such as low-interest loans, grants, or community investment models. These solutions can help reduce the upfront costs of renewable energy systems and make it easier for communities to invest in clean energy infrastructure. Additionally, energy communities can benefit from economies of scale, as pooling resources and sharing costs among members can make large projects more affordable and financially viable.

Technical challenges also pose significant barriers to the implementation of energy communities. While renewable energy technologies have become more efficient and affordable, integrating them into existing energy systems—particularly in decentralized and community-driven models—can be complex. Energy communities often need to develop and manage their own energy infrastructure, such as solar panels, wind turbines, and energy storage systems. This requires technical expertise in the design, installation, and maintenance of renewable energy systems, as well as knowledge of energy management and grid integration. In some cases, communities may lack the technical skills or resources necessary to implement and operate these systems effectively.

To overcome these technical challenges, energy communities must collaborate with skilled professionals, such as engineers and energy consultants, who can help design and implement appropriate renewable energy solutions. Additionally, governments and energy organizations can support training programs that build local expertise in renewable energy technologies, empowering communities to take control of their energy future. Investing in capacity-building initiatives can also help ensure the long-term sustainability of energy communities, as they will be better equipped to manage and maintain their energy systems over time.

Regulatory challenges are another significant barrier to the successful implementation of energy communities. In many regions, existing energy regulations are designed for centralized, utility-driven systems and may not be well-suited to accommodate decentralized energy production or collective ownership models. For example, energy communities may face difficulties in accessing the grid or receiving fair compensation for the energy they generate. Net metering policies, which allow prosumers to sell excess energy back to the grid, are not always available or may be poorly designed, limiting the financial viability of energy communities. Additionally, regulatory barriers to peer-to-peer energy trading or the establishment of community-owned energy systems may prevent communities from fully realizing the potential benefits of renewable energy.

To address these regulatory challenges, governments must develop policies and frameworks that support the growth of energy communities. This may include revising grid access rules, creating incentives for collective energy projects, and establishing clear regulations for energy trading and compensation. By providing a supportive regulatory environment, governments can help energy communities overcome barriers to implementation and create more equitable and sustainable energy systems.

Finally, community resistance to new technologies can also be a significant barrier to the adoption of energy communities. In areas where traditional energy systems are well-established, there may be skepticism or resistance to change, particularly if community members are unfamiliar with renewable energy technologies or are concerned about potential disruptions to their energy supply. This resistance can be compounded by a lack of awareness about the benefits of energy communities, such as lower energy costs, improved energy security, and environmental sustainability.

To address community resistance, it is essential to engage local residents early in the planning process and provide clear, accessible information about the benefits and challenges of energy communities. Public outreach efforts, such as workshops, informational sessions, and community meetings, can help raise awareness and build trust. Additionally, involving community members in decision-making processes and ensuring that their concerns are addressed can help foster a sense of ownership and commitment to the project.

Chapter 6: Digitalization and the Future of Energy Prosumers

As energy systems become increasingly decentralized, digital technologies are playing a pivotal role in transforming the way energy is generated, consumed, and managed. This chapter explores how digitalization is shaping the future of energy prosumers, empowering individuals and communities to optimize their energy use, enhance system integration, and participate in innovative energy markets. From the rise of smart grids and energy management platforms to the integration of blockchain and the IoT, digital tools are unlocking new opportunities for prosumers to engage in the energy transition. By examining the latest advancements in digital technology, this chapter provides a comprehensive look at how these innovations will drive the growth of energy prosumers and contribute to the development of more sustainable, resilient, and equitable energy systems in the years to come.

6.1. Role of Artificial Intelligence (AI)

AI is playing an increasingly important role in the optimization of energy systems, particularly as energy prosumers become more prevalent. Through its ability to process vast amounts of data and learn from patterns, AI helps to enhance the efficiency, reliability, and sustainability of energy consumption and production. In both residential and commercial settings, AI can optimize energy usage, predict maintenance needs, and improve grid management, contributing to the transition to decentralized, renewable energy systems.

One of the key ways AI is transforming energy systems is by optimizing energy consumption and production. AI-powered algorithms can analyze real-time data from smart meters, energy storage systems, and renewable energy sources like solar panels and wind turbines to predict energy demand and adjust energy consumption accordingly. By continuously learning from historical patterns and external factors such as weather forecasts, AI can forecast when energy production will peak or dip, enabling prosumers to adjust their usage behavior for maximum efficiency. For example, AI can automatically control heating, ventilation, and air conditioning (HVAC) systems in smart homes or businesses, adjusting settings based on occupancy, external temperature, and energy availability, ensuring optimal comfort and minimizing energy waste.

For energy prosumers, AI also plays a vital role in managing the generation of renewable energy. Solar panel output can be influenced by factors such as weather conditions, time of day, and geographic location. AI can analyze these variables and make real-time adjustments to optimize energy generation. It can also integrate energy storage systems, ensuring that excess energy produced during peak generation times is stored and used later when production is low. By optimizing both energy production and consumption, AI helps prosumers become more self-sufficient, reduce reliance on the grid, and lower overall energy costs.

Predictive analytics is another powerful application of AI in energy systems. Through predictive maintenance and grid management, AI can help prevent energy disruptions and reduce maintenance costs. By continuously monitoring the performance of energy assets—such as solar panels, wind turbines, batteries, and other equipment—AI can identify anomalies and predict potential failures before they occur. Machine learning algorithms analyze data from sensors and historical maintenance records to detect early warning signs of equipment malfunction. This allows operators to schedule maintenance proactively, minimizing downtime and reducing repair costs.

In the context of grid management, AI can also be used to predict energy demand and optimize the distribution of energy across the grid. By analyzing historical data on energy usage patterns, weather forecasts, and real-time energy production, AI can predict when and where energy demand will be highest. This allows grid operators to make informed decisions about energy distribution, ensuring that power is delivered where it is needed most. AI can also help manage fluctuations in renewable energy production, such as those caused by intermittent solar or wind power, by adjusting grid settings to accommodate these fluctuations without sacrificing stability.

AI's predictive capabilities extend beyond individual systems and equipment, as it can be applied to manage entire energy grids. In smart grids, AI can optimize the flow of electricity, balancing supply and demand while accommodating energy from multiple sources, including distributed generation from prosumers. This is particularly valuable in decentralized energy systems, where numerous small-scale generators (e.g., rooftop solar panels) may contribute to the overall supply. AI enables grid operators to efficiently manage these inputs and ensure that power is delivered reliably and cost-effectively.

6.2. Blockchain and Peer-to-Peer Trading

Blockchain technology has emerged as a powerful tool for enhancing the transparency, security, and efficiency of energy transactions. In the context of energy prosumers, blockchain is particularly valuable for facilitating P2P energy trading, allowing individuals, businesses, and communities to buy and sell renewable energy directly to one another. By enabling secure, transparent, and decentralized transactions, blockchain has the potential to further decentralize energy markets, reducing reliance on traditional utility companies and empowering prosumers to participate more actively in energy generation, distribution, and consumption.

One of the primary benefits of blockchain technology in energy transactions is its ability to enhance transparency and trust. Blockchain operates as a decentralized, immutable ledger, meaning that once a transaction is recorded, it cannot be altered or tampered with. This ensures that all parties involved in an energy transaction have access to the same information, creating a transparent and trustworthy record of energy exchanges. In the context of P2P energy trading, this is particularly important, as it helps build confidence between buyers and sellers. Both parties can verify the energy transaction in real-time, ensuring that the energy transferred is accurately accounted for and that the terms of the trade are met. This transparency also reduces the potential for disputes and fraud, as the blockchain ledger provides an auditable trail of transactions that is publicly accessible to all participants.

In addition to increasing transparency, blockchain can help streamline energy trading by automating transactions through **smart contracts**. Smart contracts are self-executing contracts with the terms of the agreement directly written into code. These contracts automatically execute when predefined conditions are met, removing the need for intermediaries and reducing transaction costs. For example, in a P2P energy transaction, a smart contract can automatically transfer payment from the buyer to the seller once the agreed-upon amount of energy is delivered, eliminating the need for a central authority or third-party mediator. This not only improves the efficiency of energy trading but also ensures that transactions are completed quickly and without unnecessary delays.

Blockchain's ability to facilitate decentralized energy markets is another key advantage. Traditional energy systems are highly centralized, with large utility companies controlling the production, distribution, and sale of electricity. This model often results in inefficiencies, high costs, and limited options for consumers. Blockchain enables the decentralization of energy markets by allowing prosumers to trade energy directly with one another, bypassing traditional intermediaries such as utility companies. This peer-to-peer energy trading system opens up new market opportunities for prosumers, enabling them to sell excess energy generated from renewable sources like solar panels or wind turbines to neighbors or local businesses. This decentralization increases market competition, which can drive down energy prices, encourage innovation, and promote the adoption of renewable energy technologies.

Furthermore, blockchain can help integrate DERs into the broader energy market. As more prosumers generate their own renewable energy, the grid becomes increasingly decentralized, with power coming from many small, distributed sources rather than a few large plants. Blockchain facilitates the management of this complex system by enabling secure, real-time transactions between multiple energy producers and consumers. This creates a more flexible, resilient, and scalable energy market, where prosumers can participate more directly in the energy economy and contribute to the stability and efficiency of the grid.

The potential of blockchain to decentralize energy markets further extends to the creation of **VPPs**. VPPs aggregate the energy generated by multiple small-scale prosumers into a single, flexible energy resource that can be used to balance supply and demand across the grid. By using blockchain to manage the transactions and coordination between prosumers in a VPP, the system can operate without the need for a central authority, making it more efficient and cost-effective.

6.3. The IoT

The IoT is revolutionizing the way energy systems are managed, offering a range of technologies that enable energy prosumers to optimize their energy production, consumption, and storage. By connecting everyday devices to the internet, IoT creates a network of smart devices that can communicate with one another and with central systems, providing real-time data and enabling greater control over energy use. This section explores the role of smart devices in enabling prosumption, focusing on how IoT enhances the efficiency of energy systems, and addresses the challenges related to interoperability between different devices and platforms.

Smart devices are at the heart of IoT applications in the energy sector. These devices include smart meters, thermostats, lighting systems, appliances, and energy storage systems, all of which are capable of collecting and transmitting data about energy consumption, production, and system performance. Smart meters, for example, allow prosumers to track their energy usage in real time, providing insights into patterns of consumption. This enables users to adjust their behaviors to minimize energy waste, such as turning off appliances when they are not in use or adjusting thermostat settings to optimize heating and cooling. By providing detailed feedback on energy use, smart meters empower consumers to make informed decisions about energy management, leading to more efficient use of resources.

In addition to monitoring consumption, smart thermostats and other energy management systems can autonomously adjust energy settings based on user preferences, weather conditions, and real-time data. For instance, a smart thermostat can learn from user behavior and adjust the temperature settings of a home to optimize comfort while minimizing energy consumption. By integrating these devices with renewable energy systems, such as solar panels or wind turbines, prosumers can further optimize their energy usage. When excess energy is generated, it can be stored in batteries or used to power energy-intensive appliances during peak production times. Conversely, during periods of low energy production, IoT systems can automatically adjust energy consumption to reduce reliance on the grid, enhancing energy self-sufficiency.

IoT also plays a critical role in enabling energy storage systems to operate efficiently. With the use of IoT-enabled sensors and controllers, energy storage systems can monitor battery levels, charge and discharge cycles, and energy flow, allowing for more efficient use of stored energy. These systems can be programmed to charge during periods of low energy demand or when renewable energy production is high, and discharge when demand spikes or when renewable generation is low. By integrating IoT with energy storage solutions, prosumers can maximize their use of renewable energy, reducing reliance on traditional grid power and lowering energy costs.

One of the key benefits of IoT in prosumer energy systems is its ability to enhance grid management and coordination. Smart devices within a prosumer's energy system are capable of communicating with the broader grid through smart grids. This allows for real-time monitoring and adjustments to energy distribution, ensuring that supply matches demand. IoT-enabled smart grids can detect imbalances in energy supply and demand and optimize energy flow to prevent blackouts or overloading of the grid. For instance, during periods of high renewable energy production, excess energy generated by prosumers can be distributed efficiently across the grid, while during peak demand periods, smart grids can ensure that energy is allocated where it is most needed.

However, one of the main challenges associated with the integration of IoT in energy systems is interoperability. With a wide range of smart devices, sensors, and platforms available on the market, ensuring that these technologies can work seamlessly together is a significant hurdle. Different manufacturers may use proprietary communication protocols or data formats, making it difficult to integrate devices from various sources into a cohesive, unified system. This lack of interoperability can create inefficiencies, as users may be unable to optimize their energy systems fully if their devices cannot communicate effectively with one another.

To address interoperability challenges, industry standards and protocols must be established to ensure that IoT devices can communicate with each other across different platforms. Efforts are underway to develop open standards that promote compatibility and enable different devices and systems to work together. For example, the OpenADR (Automated Demand Response) standard allows IoT-enabled devices to communicate with energy management systems and the grid, enabling more efficient demand-side management. Similarly, Zigbee and Wi-Fi are two commonly used wireless communication protocols that are designed to ensure compatibility between smart devices. These standards help create a more integrated IoT ecosystem, allowing prosumers to use a range of devices from different manufacturers while still benefiting from seamless operation and optimization.

Another solution to interoperability issues is the development of smart hubs and platforms that act as intermediaries between different devices and systems. These platforms aggregate data from multiple smart devices, translate different communication protocols, and provide a single interface for managing energy systems. By using smart hubs or cloud-based platforms, prosumers can easily monitor and control their devices, even if they come from different manufacturers or use different technologies. This simplifies the process of integrating IoT-enabled devices into a prosumer energy system and ensures that users can maximize the benefits of their technology.

6.4. Future Trends in Digital Energy Systems

The future of energy systems is increasingly digital, with advancements in technologies such as the IoT, 5G, and AI driving the transition toward more efficient, flexible, and decentralized energy networks. One of the key trends shaping the future of energy systems is the integration of prosumer technologies with the development of smart cities. Additionally, the rollout of 5G technology and beyond holds the potential to further enhance the capabilities of digital energy systems, enabling real-time communication, improved grid management, and greater integration of renewable energy sources. This section explores the integration of prosumer technologies with smart cities and the implications of 5G and future wireless technologies for energy systems.

The integration of prosumer technologies with smart cities is one of the most promising developments in the future of energy systems. Smart cities use advanced digital technologies to manage urban infrastructure, improve efficiency, and enhance the quality of life for residents. By integrating renewable energy systems, energy storage, and IoT-enabled devices, smart cities can optimize energy consumption and create more sustainable, resilient urban environments. Prosumer technologies, such as rooftop solar panels, wind turbines, and battery storage, can play a central role in this integration by allowing individuals, businesses, and communities to generate and manage their own energy.

In a smart city, prosumer-generated energy can be seamlessly integrated into the city's broader energy network, creating a decentralized energy system that is more resilient and flexible. For example, renewable energy produced by prosumers can be shared through a local energy market or virtual power plant (VPP), where excess energy is traded between individuals, businesses, and the grid. This integration can help balance supply and demand in real time, reduce strain on centralized energy infrastructure, and increase the overall efficiency of the energy system. In addition, smart cities can use digital platforms to monitor energy consumption and production, providing real-time insights that allow city planners and residents to optimize energy use and reduce waste.

Furthermore, smart city infrastructure can be designed to accommodate and support prosumer technologies. Smart grids, for example, can manage the bidirectional flow of energy, enabling energy to be sent from prosumers to the grid and vice versa. In a smart city, the energy grid is dynamic and can respond to fluctuations in supply and demand, ensuring that energy is distributed efficiently and cost-effectively. This type of energy management is made possible by the integration of IoT sensors, AI, and other digital technologies that enable real-time monitoring and control of energy systems. By incorporating prosumer-generated energy into the broader urban energy infrastructure, smart cities can help reduce greenhouse gas emissions, lower energy costs, and promote energy independence.

The advent of 5G technology is another key factor that will shape the future of digital energy systems. 5G, the fifth generation of mobile telecommunications technology, offers significant improvements over previous generations in terms of speed, capacity, and latency. These advancements have profound implications for energy systems, particularly in terms of enabling faster and more efficient communication between devices, sensors, and control systems. The increased bandwidth and lower latency of 5G networks will allow for real-time data transmission and more responsive energy management.

For prosumers, 5G technology will enhance the performance and capabilities of smart devices, such as smart meters, energy storage systems, and renewable energy generators. With faster data transmission, prosumers will be able to receive real-time updates on their energy usage and production, allowing them to make more informed decisions about energy consumption and storage. In addition, 5G will enable more seamless communication between energy devices, creating a more integrated and coordinated energy system. For example, energy storage systems can be dynamically adjusted based on real-time energy production from solar panels, ensuring that excess energy is stored when available and used efficiently when needed.

On a larger scale, the deployment of 5G will improve the management of smart grids and enable more sophisticated grid services, such as demand response and real-time energy trading. With the ability to transmit large volumes of data quickly and securely, 5G will enable grid operators to monitor energy supply and demand in real time, adjusting energy distribution as needed to maintain grid stability. This will help integrate renewable energy sources, which are often variable, into the grid, ensuring that the energy system can accommodate fluctuations in production without sacrificing reliability.

Looking beyond 5G, future wireless technologies such as 6G and beyond are expected to further enhance the capabilities of energy systems. These next-generation technologies will offer even greater data speeds, lower latency, and more robust connectivity, enabling even more sophisticated energy management and control. For example, 6G could facilitate the integration of autonomous systems, such as electric vehicles and drones, into the energy grid, allowing for more dynamic energy distribution and storage. Additionally, as AI and machine learning algorithms become more advanced, the combination of high-speed wireless networks and AI will enable predictive analytics that can anticipate energy demand, optimize energy production, and even forecast energy price fluctuations.

Chapter 7: Prosumers and the Energy Transition

The role of energy prosumers is central to the global transition toward a more sustainable and decentralized energy system. As individuals and communities increasingly take control of their energy production, consumption, and storage, they become key players in the shift from fossil fuel dependence to renewable energy sources. This chapter explores how prosumers are driving the energy transition, examining the key benefits and challenges of prosumption in this context. It highlights the ways in which prosumers contribute to reducing carbon emissions, enhancing energy resilience, and fostering a more equitable energy landscape. Additionally, the chapter discusses the policy, technological, and social innovations required to empower prosumers and ensure that the energy transition is inclusive, efficient, and sustainable for all.

7.1. Prosumers in the Context of Climate Change

Energy prosumers play an increasingly important role in mitigating climate change by contributing to the reduction of greenhouse gas (GHG) emissions and supporting the achievement of international climate targets. As individuals and communities take ownership of their energy production, consumption, and storage, they are actively participating in the transition to a more sustainable and low-carbon energy system. Through the adoption of renewable energy technologies, energy efficiency practices, and the decentralization of energy systems, prosumers help reduce the reliance on fossil fuels and lower overall carbon emissions, playing a critical part in global efforts to combat climate change.

One of the most direct ways in which prosumers contribute to GHG emissions reduction is through the generation of renewable energy. By installing solar panels, wind turbines, or other renewable energy systems, prosumers reduce their reliance on fossil fuels, which are the primary source of carbon emissions in the energy sector. Solar and wind energy, for example, are virtually carbon-neutral energy sources, as their production does not involve the burning of fossil fuels. As more prosumers adopt these technologies, the overall demand for fossil fuel-generated electricity decreases, contributing to a reduction in the carbon intensity of the energy grid. This shift towards renewable energy generation at the individual and community levels helps lower GHG emissions, making a tangible contribution to efforts to reduce global carbon footprints.

Prosumers can also reduce emissions through energy storage and energy efficiency. Energy storage systems, such as batteries, allow prosumers to store excess renewable energy generated during times of high production (e.g., during sunny or windy periods) for later use. This reduces the need to rely on conventional, fossil-fuel-based electricity during periods of low renewable energy generation. Additionally, by integrating smart devices and energy management systems, prosumers can optimize their energy usage, reducing waste and improving efficiency. Smart thermostats, lighting systems, and energy-efficient appliances all contribute to minimizing energy consumption and, consequently, GHG emissions. These actions, taken by individual households and communities, collectively reduce overall energy demand and increase the efficiency of the energy system.

In the broader context of climate change mitigation, prosumers are crucial in helping countries and regions meet their international climate targets. The Paris Agreement, adopted in 2015, set ambitious goals to limit global temperature rise to well below 2°C, with efforts to limit it to 1.5°C. Achieving these goals requires a dramatic reduction in global GHG emissions, with the energy sector playing a central role in the transition. As prosumers increase their share of renewable energy generation and consumption, they contribute to the decarbonization of the energy sector, which is the largest source of global emissions. The more prosumers participate in this transition, the greater the potential for meeting national and international climate goals, reducing the reliance on fossil fuels and accelerating the global shift towards clean energy.

Moreover, prosumers can support international climate targets by helping to decentralize energy systems. Centralized energy production, often dependent on fossil fuels, has significant environmental impacts. By decentralizing energy generation, prosumers can promote the use of clean, renewable energy sources closer to where energy is consumed, reducing transmission losses and minimizing the environmental impact of large-scale power generation. This decentralization, combined with the adoption of renewable energy technologies, brings nations closer to achieving their carbon neutrality objectives.

7.2. Decarbonization and Decentralization

The energy transition, driven by the need for decarbonization and decentralization, aligns closely with the rise of prosumer models. By empowering individuals and communities to generate, store, and manage their own renewable energy, prosumer models support the broader goal of reducing carbon emissions while reshaping energy systems to be more decentralized and sustainable. This section explores the synergies between the energy transition and prosumer models, as well as the challenges in achieving a just transition that ensures equitable access to the benefits of decarbonization and decentralization.

One of the primary synergies between decarbonization and prosumer models is the ability to reduce GHG emissions. Prosumers typically generate energy from renewable sources, such as solar panels, wind turbines, and small-scale hydroelectric systems, which do not produce carbon emissions when generating electricity. By shifting energy production away from fossil fuel-based power plants toward locally generated renewable energy, prosumer models help decarbonize the energy sector. This shift not only contributes to global efforts to mitigate climate change but also reduces reliance on centralized power generation, which often relies on carbon-intensive sources of energy such as coal and natural gas.

The decentralization of energy systems is another critical aspect of the synergy between prosumer models and decarbonization. Traditionally, the energy system has been highly centralized, with large power plants generating electricity and transmitting it to consumers through extensive networks of power lines. This model, while effective in providing reliable power, is associated with inefficiencies, transmission losses, and a high environmental footprint. Prosumers, by generating energy locally, reduce the need for long-distance electricity transmission and contribute to a more resilient and efficient energy grid. Decentralized systems are also more adaptable, as they allow for the integration of diverse renewable energy sources, such as rooftop solar, community wind farms, and localized battery storage, which enhance grid stability and flexibility. This shift toward decentralized energy production aligns with broader goals of reducing carbon emissions while also increasing the reliability and resilience of energy systems.

In addition to decarbonization and decentralization, prosumer models can drive energy equity by providing communities with more control over their energy resources. Prosumers can participate in local energy markets, where they can sell excess energy back to the grid or trade with neighbors, creating opportunities for financial gains and reducing energy costs. This model empowers communities to become more energy self-sufficient, particularly in areas where traditional energy infrastructure is lacking or where energy access is limited. By promoting the use of renewable energy and creating more localized energy systems, prosumer models can help achieve a more just and equitable energy transition.

However, achieving a just transition to decarbonized and decentralized energy systems is not without challenges. One of the key barriers to a just transition is the issue of affordability and access to renewable energy technologies. While the cost of renewable energy technologies has declined in recent years, the upfront costs of installing solar panels, wind turbines, and energy storage systems remain a significant barrier for many low-income households and communities. Without access to financial incentives, subsidies, or low-interest loans, these communities may be excluded from the benefits of prosumer models and continue to rely on fossil fuels or expensive grid electricity. To ensure a just transition, policies must be designed to make renewable energy technologies more affordable and accessible to all, particularly those in underserved and marginalized communities.

Another challenge is the uneven distribution of benefits from decentralization. While some communities may benefit from lower energy costs, increased energy independence, and local economic opportunities, others may struggle to access these advantages. For example, rural or remote communities with limited access to grid infrastructure may face difficulties in adopting renewable energy technologies due to geographic isolation, a lack of local expertise, or insufficient resources. Similarly, wealthier households and businesses are more likely to be able to invest in renewable energy systems, leaving lower-income households without the financial means to participate in prosumer models. Addressing these disparities will require targeted policies that ensure the benefits of the energy transition are shared equitably, such as community-based renewable energy projects, income-based subsidies, and training programs that build local capacity.

7.3. Global Examples of Prosumption in Action

Energy prosumption has taken many forms across the world, with diverse cultural and regional approaches reflecting varying levels of technological development, political priorities, and social contexts. From grassroots community projects to advanced, large-scale integrations of prosumer technologies, these initiatives are proving that decentralized energy systems can work in a variety of settings. This section highlights examples of prosumption in action, drawing lessons from successful initiatives around the globe that showcase the potential and challenges of implementing prosumer models.

One of the most well-known global examples of prosumption is found in Germany. The country's Energiewende, or energy transition, has focused on promoting renewable energy, increasing energy efficiency, and decentralizing energy production. Germany's feed-in tariff (FIT) system, which was introduced in the early 2000s, provided financial incentives for individuals and businesses to install solar panels, wind turbines, and other renewable energy systems. This policy allowed Germany to become one of the leaders in solar energy adoption, with over 1.5 million solar installations across the country by 2020. Prosumers in Germany benefit from the ability to generate their own electricity, with excess energy fed back into the grid in exchange for payments or credits. This model has not only helped reduce the country's reliance on fossil fuels but has also created a robust market for renewable energy technology, driving innovation and job creation. The success of Germany's FIT policy shows how government support and clear regulatory frameworks can encourage widespread adoption of prosumer technologies and accelerate the transition to clean energy.

In the United States, states like California and Hawaii have pioneered prosumer models through the implementation of net metering policies. Net metering allows prosumers to feed excess electricity from their renewable energy systems back into the grid, receiving credit for the energy they generate. This policy has been particularly successful in California, where the combination of high solar potential, supportive policies, and relatively high electricity prices has led to significant adoption of residential solar energy. In Hawaii, the decentralized adoption of solar power has played a key role in reducing the state's dependence on imported fossil fuels, which had been a significant economic and environmental concern. Prosumers in these regions benefit from reduced energy costs and greater energy independence, while also contributing to the broader energy transition by generating clean power. These initiatives highlight the importance of supportive policies that incentivize prosumer participation and the role that local conditions—such as access to renewable resources—play in shaping the success of prosumer models.

In Denmark, community-owned wind farms represent another model of prosumer engagement in the energy transition. Denmark is a leader in wind energy production, and the country has long embraced decentralized energy systems. Many small communities and cooperatives have banded together to invest in wind turbines, allowing residents to collectively own and profit from the energy generated. This model provides economic benefits to local communities, helps reduce their carbon footprints, and strengthens social bonds by involving people in energy decisions. Denmark's success with community-owned wind energy has been driven by favorable government policies, including grants, subsidies, and access to financing for small-scale renewable energy projects. The lessons from Denmark's experience underscore the importance of community involvement and local ownership in fostering long-term sustainability and engagement in renewable energy initiatives.

India provides another example of prosumer models adapted to local contexts. In rural areas where access to the national grid is limited or unreliable, solar-powered microgrids have been implemented to provide electricity to off-grid communities. These microgrids, often owned and operated by local communities, provide power for basic needs like lighting, water pumping, and small-scale business operations. Prosumers in these areas contribute to the generation and distribution of solar energy, benefiting from reliable electricity while reducing their reliance on costly and polluting diesel generators. These microgrids not only provide energy access to underserved communities but also promote local economic development by enabling small businesses to thrive and by improving educational opportunities through reliable power for schools and healthcare facilities. India's experience highlights the potential for prosumer models to address energy poverty and promote equitable access to clean energy in developing regions.

In Australia, a more recent prosumer initiative is the Solar Gardens program. This program allows individuals who cannot install solar panels on their own properties—such as renters or those with unsuitable roofs—to participate in solar energy production by subscribing to a community solar project. Solar gardens are typically large-scale solar installations located in a central location, with energy subscribers receiving a share of the electricity generated. This model has gained popularity in Australia as a way to expand access to renewable energy for those who do not have the physical infrastructure to install solar panels. The Solar Gardens program exemplifies the importance of ensuring that all individuals, regardless of property ownership or other constraints, can participate in the energy transition.

These global examples highlight diverse cultural and regional approaches to prosumption, each shaped by local resources, policy frameworks, and community needs. The successful initiatives from Germany, the United States, Denmark, India, and Australia demonstrate that prosumer models can take many forms, from individual solar installations to community-based energy projects. They also show that the key to success lies in creating supportive policy environments, ensuring equitable access to renewable energy technologies, and fostering community engagement.

The lessons learned from these initiatives emphasize several key factors for the successful implementation of prosumer models. First, strong policy frameworks and financial incentives are essential for encouraging adoption. Second, local community involvement and ownership of energy projects can strengthen social cohesion and ensure the long-term sustainability of renewable energy systems. Finally, innovative solutions, such as community solar programs and microgrids, can expand access to renewable energy for underserved populations and ensure that the benefits of prosumption are widely distributed.

7.4. Opportunities for Scalability

Energy prosumption, which involves individuals and communities generating, managing, and consuming their own energy, presents numerous opportunities for scalability. As the energy transition progresses, expanding from local to regional energy networks and leveraging technology to bridge urban-rural divides will be critical to realizing the full potential of prosumer models. This section examines the opportunities for scaling up prosumer initiatives, including the expansion of local energy systems into regional networks and the role of technology in overcoming geographical and infrastructural barriers to energy access.

One of the primary opportunities for scalability in energy prosumption is the expansion from local energy systems to larger regional networks. Initially, prosumer energy systems tend to be small-scale, with individual households or communities generating their own renewable energy through systems like solar panels, wind turbines, or microgrids. However, by connecting these localized energy systems into broader regional networks, it is possible to create a more integrated and resilient energy infrastructure. This regionalization of energy systems can facilitate the efficient distribution of energy, optimize energy storage and sharing, and balance supply and demand across a larger area.

A key advantage of scaling up to regional networks is the ability to integrate energy production from multiple prosumers into a cohesive system. For example, in a local setting, individual energy production might be inconsistent due to fluctuations in renewable energy sources such as solar or wind. However, by expanding to a regional level, areas with high solar production can support regions with low solar availability, creating a more stable and reliable energy system. This integration allows prosumers to contribute to the overall energy mix and ensures that energy is distributed where it is needed most. Moreover, regional networks can incorporate advanced grid technologies, such as smart grids, to better manage the distribution of energy, allowing for real-time adjustments to match supply with demand.

A key example of this scalability is the development of VPPs, which aggregate DERs from prosumers to create a larger, more flexible energy system. VPPs enable prosumers to share their surplus energy with other participants in the network, thereby enhancing the efficiency and reliability of the energy system. By expanding these networks to a regional level, VPPs can help optimize energy flow, reduce energy waste, and support grid stability, while also providing financial benefits to prosumers who participate in the trading and sharing of energy.

In addition to expanding local energy systems into regional networks, technology plays a crucial role in bridging the gap between urban and rural areas, addressing disparities in energy access and infrastructure. Urban areas typically have better access to energy infrastructure, including reliable electricity grids and advanced energy technologies. In contrast, rural and remote areas often face challenges in accessing reliable, affordable, and clean energy. Prosumers in these areas may lack the necessary infrastructure to generate, store, or distribute energy, which limits their ability to participate in the energy transition.

One way to overcome these barriers is by leveraging smart technologies and IoT-enabled devices that allow for decentralized energy management in both urban and rural areas. For example, smart grids and microgrids can be implemented in rural areas to provide localized energy solutions that are less dependent on centralized power sources. These technologies enable rural communities to manage their own energy generation and consumption, often relying on renewable sources like solar or wind, while maintaining the ability to connect to larger grids when necessary. In these rural microgrids, prosumers can produce and store renewable energy, reducing reliance on fossil fuels and increasing energy security.

Another technological solution for bridging the urban-rural divide is energy storage systems, which allow prosumers in remote areas to store excess energy generated during peak production times for later use. For example, solar energy generated during the day can be stored in batteries and used at night when the sun is not shining. By incorporating storage systems into rural prosumer models, these communities can become more self-sufficient and reduce their dependence on unreliable or expensive grid electricity. Additionally, energy storage can enhance grid stability, as surplus energy generated in one area can be stored and redistributed to meet demand in other areas.

The internet and mobile technology are also key enablers in scaling prosumer initiatives. In rural regions where access to energy infrastructure may be limited, mobile applications and cloud-based platforms can facilitate the management of energy systems. Through these platforms, rural prosumers can monitor their energy production and consumption, participate in energy markets, and share excess energy with others. These platforms also allow rural areas to connect with urban markets, providing greater opportunities for trade and exchange of renewable energy.

Another promising solution is the development of community energy projects, which can serve as a bridge between urban and rural areas. In these projects, urban investors or organizations can partner with rural communities to fund and develop renewable energy systems that benefit both parties. For example, a rural community could generate renewable energy through a solar farm or wind turbine, while urban areas could provide funding, expertise, and access to markets. These partnerships enable rural communities to gain access to the resources they need to develop prosumer models, while also allowing urban areas to expand their renewable energy capacity and support more sustainable development.

Chapter 8: Challenges and Barriers for Prosumers

While the role of prosumers in the energy transition is pivotal, their widespread adoption and integration into energy systems are not without challenges. This chapter explores the various barriers that limit the potential of prosumer models, from financial constraints and technical limitations to regulatory hurdles and societal resistance. It examines the complexities of accessing renewable energy technologies, the infrastructure required to support prosumers, and the policy frameworks necessary to incentivize participation. Additionally, the chapter delves into the social and cultural challenges that may hinder prosumer engagement, addressing concerns related to equity, fairness, and community involvement. By identifying these challenges, this chapter aims to provide a comprehensive understanding of the obstacles facing prosumers and offer insights into how they can be overcome to create a more inclusive, sustainable energy future.

8.1. Technical Challenges

As energy prosumers play an increasingly central role in the transition to decentralized and renewable energy systems, a range of technical challenges must be addressed to fully unlock the potential of prosumer models. Among the most significant hurdles are issues related to grid integration and intermittency, as well as the need for ongoing maintenance and technical support for renewable energy technologies. Addressing these technical barriers is essential to ensuring the smooth operation and sustainability of prosumer-driven energy systems.

One of the primary technical challenges faced by prosumers is integrating decentralized renewable energy production, such as solar and wind power, into the existing grid infrastructure. Renewable energy sources are inherently variable, with solar power generation dependent on sunlight and wind power generation influenced by wind conditions. This intermittency poses significant challenges for grid operators, as the amount of energy being produced by prosumers can fluctuate throughout the day and across seasons. When renewable energy generation exceeds demand, excess energy may be wasted, whereas, during periods of low renewable generation, additional energy may need to be drawn from conventional fossil-fuel-based sources, which can be inefficient and environmentally damaging.

To address these intermittency issues, grids need to be upgraded and made more flexible to accommodate the integration of renewable energy. Smart grids and energy storage systems are essential components of this solution. Smart grids enable real-time communication between prosumers, grid operators, and energy systems, allowing for better management of energy flows and ensuring that renewable energy is used efficiently. For example, during periods of excess energy generation, smart grids can direct surplus energy to energy storage systems, where it can be stored for later use when generation is low. Similarly, during periods of high demand, the grid can tap into stored energy to supplement renewable energy production.

While these solutions are promising, they require significant investment in infrastructure, both in terms of upgrading grid systems and installing advanced energy storage technologies. These systems must be capable of handling bidirectional energy flows, where energy can move from the grid to prosumers and vice versa, while ensuring that the grid remains stable and reliable.

Another technical challenge for prosumers is the maintenance and technical support required for renewable energy systems. The widespread adoption of renewable energy technologies, such as solar panels, wind turbines, and battery storage systems, introduces the need for ongoing upkeep, monitoring, and troubleshooting. Unlike traditional energy systems, which are often managed by large utilities with dedicated maintenance teams, prosumers are typically responsible for the maintenance of their own energy systems. For many individuals and communities, this can be a daunting task, particularly for those with limited technical expertise or resources.

Solar panels, for example, require regular cleaning to ensure optimal performance, while wind turbines may need periodic inspections to prevent mechanical failure. Energy storage systems also require monitoring to ensure that batteries are operating at peak efficiency and that they are properly charged and discharged to maximize their lifespan. Without proper maintenance, the efficiency and longevity of renewable energy systems can be compromised, reducing the overall economic and environmental benefits for prosumers.

Additionally, many prosumers may face challenges in accessing reliable technical support, particularly in rural or underserved areas. In regions with limited access to qualified technicians or service providers, prosumers may struggle to find the expertise needed to troubleshoot and repair their systems. This lack of support can be a barrier to the adoption of renewable energy technologies, as potential prosumers may be deterred by concerns about ongoing maintenance or the difficulty of finding professional help when needed.

To overcome these barriers, it is essential to build technical support infrastructure that can cater to the needs of prosumers. This includes providing access to training programs and certifications that enable individuals to acquire the skills needed to maintain their systems independently. It also involves developing partnerships with service providers who can offer regular maintenance and support, particularly in remote or underserved areas. Additionally, manufacturers and installers of renewable energy technologies can play a role by offering comprehensive warranties and remote monitoring services to ensure that systems are operating efficiently and that potential issues can be addressed before they become major problems.

8.2. Economic Barriers

Despite the significant environmental and economic benefits that energy prosumers can offer, several economic barriers hinder their widespread adoption and integration into the energy market. Among the most prominent challenges are high upfront costs and difficulties related to financing renewable energy technologies. Additionally, ensuring a fair and competitive market for all energy participants, particularly in regions where prosumer models are emerging, is critical to ensuring that these systems are equitable, accessible, and sustainable. Addressing these economic barriers is crucial to accelerating the growth of prosumer-driven energy systems.

One of the most significant economic barriers to prosumer adoption is the high initial cost of renewable energy systems, such as solar panels, wind turbines, and energy storage solutions. While the costs of these technologies have decreased significantly over the past decade, the upfront investment required for installation remains a substantial hurdle for many individuals and communities. For example, installing a solar panel system, including the cost of the panels, inverters, batteries, and installation, can cost several thousand dollars. For low- and middle-income households, as well as small businesses, this initial cost can be prohibitively expensive, even if the long-term savings are substantial.

The financing of renewable energy systems also presents challenges, particularly for those without access to capital or credit. Many prosumers rely on loans, incentives, or grants to help cover the costs of installation, but these financial products may not always be available or accessible, especially in underserved or rural areas. In some cases, financial institutions may be reluctant to offer loans for renewable energy systems due to perceived risks, lack of collateral, or limited knowledge of the sector. Without access to affordable financing, many potential prosumers may be unable to participate in the energy transition, despite the potential long-term economic benefits.

To address these barriers, it is crucial to develop financial mechanisms that make renewable energy technologies more accessible. Governments and private financial institutions can offer low-interest loans, tax credits, subsidies, or grants to reduce the financial burden on prosumers. Innovative financing models, such as solar leasing, PPAs, or community solar programs, can also make it easier for households and businesses to invest in renewable energy systems without bearing the full upfront costs. These models allow prosumers to share costs, generate savings, and make energy systems more affordable and accessible.

Another key economic barrier to the success of prosumer models is ensuring a fair and transparent market for all energy participants. As more individuals and communities become prosumers, energy markets must be structured in a way that supports their participation without creating an uneven playing field. In many traditional energy systems, utilities and large energy corporations hold significant market power, controlling pricing, energy distribution, and access to infrastructure. Prosumers, particularly in the early stages of market development, may face challenges in gaining equal access to the energy market and ensuring that they receive fair compensation for the energy they generate and contribute.

A critical issue in ensuring fairness is net metering, which compensates prosumers for the excess energy they feed back into the grid. While net metering policies are widely used in many regions, they are often not standardized, and compensation rates can vary significantly. In some cases, prosumers may be compensated at a rate lower than the retail price of electricity, which can discourage participation and undermine the economic incentives for renewable energy adoption. In areas where grid access is limited or where prosumers face additional fees or penalties for connecting to the grid, the market may be skewed against decentralized energy production.

To create a fair and inclusive market, it is essential to develop policies that ensure prosumers are compensated fairly for the energy they generate and share. This may include revising net metering policies to reflect the true value of distributed energy and implementing transparent pricing structures that incentivize renewable energy adoption. Additionally, regulatory frameworks must address issues such as grid access, transmission fees, and the integration of renewable energy into existing infrastructure. By ensuring that prosumers are treated equitably in the energy market, policymakers can foster a more competitive and inclusive energy system that benefits all participants.

8.3. Social and Behavioral Challenges

As the energy transition progresses, social and behavioral challenges play a significant role in determining the pace and success of prosumer adoption. Although renewable energy technologies have become more accessible, their integration into daily life faces resistance from individuals and communities due to factors such as inertia, a lack of awareness, and cultural attitudes towards energy consumption. Additionally, generational and cultural divides can further complicate efforts to engage diverse populations in the shift to decentralized energy systems. Overcoming these social and behavioral challenges is essential to ensuring the success of prosumer models and the widespread adoption of renewable energy solutions.

One of the primary social challenges in the adoption of prosumer models is resistance to change. Energy consumption patterns are deeply ingrained in society, and many individuals and communities are accustomed to centralized, grid-based systems that provide reliable, consistent energy. The idea of shifting from passive consumption to active participation in energy production and management can seem daunting, particularly for individuals who have limited understanding of renewable energy technologies or the potential benefits of prosumption. As a result, many people may be hesitant to invest in renewable energy systems, either due to a lack of familiarity with the technologies or concerns about the financial and technical aspects of installation and maintenance.

This resistance to change is compounded by a lack of awareness about the environmental and economic advantages of prosumer models. Many individuals are not fully aware of the environmental impact of their energy consumption or the potential to reduce their carbon footprint by adopting renewable energy technologies. Similarly, the financial benefits of prosumption, such as reduced energy costs and the ability to sell excess energy back to the grid, may not be immediately obvious to all potential prosumers. Without adequate education and outreach, people may remain unaware of the opportunities available to them, hindering the growth of prosumer energy systems.

To overcome resistance to change, it is essential to provide clear, accessible information about the benefits of prosumption and the technologies involved. Public awareness campaigns, educational programs, and community outreach efforts can help raise awareness and dispel myths about renewable energy. Providing demonstrations of successful prosumer projects and offering case studies of individuals or communities that have successfully transitioned to renewable energy can help build confidence in the technology and encourage adoption. Additionally, simplifying the process of installation and maintenance through user-friendly systems and clear financial incentives can make it easier for people to embrace the change.

Another significant social challenge to prosumer adoption is addressing the generational and cultural divides that exist in many societies. Different generations may have varying attitudes toward energy consumption, technology adoption, and environmental responsibility. For example, younger generations, who are often more engaged with technology and more concerned about environmental issues, may be more inclined to adopt renewable energy technologies and participate in prosumer models. In contrast, older generations may be more resistant to change, particularly if they have long-standing relationships with traditional energy systems or are less familiar with new technologies.

Cultural attitudes towards energy consumption also play a crucial role in determining how willing individuals and communities are to engage with renewable energy systems. In some cultures, energy consumption is viewed as a collective responsibility, with an emphasis on shared resources and communal well-being, which may encourage collective prosumer efforts. In other cultures, however, energy consumption may be viewed more as an individual or private matter, which can limit the willingness to participate in collective energy solutions such as community solar or cooperative wind farms.

Addressing these generational and cultural divides requires tailored approaches that recognize the specific attitudes and values of different groups. For younger generations, educational campaigns and social media outreach can be effective tools for promoting prosumer models and highlighting their environmental and financial benefits. Additionally, appealing to younger consumers' desire for energy independence and control over their energy use can help encourage prosumer adoption.

For older generations, it may be necessary to focus on the practical benefits of renewable energy, such as cost savings, energy security, and the ability to reduce reliance on the grid. Providing simple, easy-to-understand resources that demystify renewable energy technologies and offering support for installation and maintenance can help reduce barriers to adoption. Encouraging intergenerational collaboration, where younger and older generations work together on energy projects, can also help bridge the divide and foster a sense of shared responsibility.

Cultural divides can be addressed through inclusive and culturally sensitive approaches that emphasize the shared benefits of renewable energy systems for communities. In areas with strong community ties, promoting collective ownership models, such as community energy cooperatives or shared solar programs, can resonate with cultural values of mutual support and shared resources. In other settings, where individual ownership may be more prevalent, promoting the benefits of personal energy independence and financial savings can help create alignment with local values and preferences.

Finally, addressing social and behavioral challenges also requires policy support that incentivizes prosumer participation across generations and cultures. Policies that provide financial incentives, simplify regulatory processes, and offer targeted support for underrepresented communities can help create an inclusive environment for prosumer adoption. Additionally, integrating renewable energy education into school curricula and community programs can help foster a culture of sustainability and encourage future generations to embrace renewable energy technologies from an early age.

8.4. Policy and Regulatory Hurdles

While energy prosumers have the potential to drive significant change in the global energy landscape, they face a variety of policy and regulatory hurdles that can hinder their widespread adoption. Navigating complex legal frameworks and regulatory environments, which often favor centralized energy systems, presents significant challenges. Additionally, overcoming political resistance to change, especially in regions with entrenched fossil fuel interests or where renewable energy policies are still in development, complicates the integration of prosumer models into existing energy systems. Addressing these challenges is essential to enable the growth of decentralized, renewable energy systems and ensure that prosumers can participate equitably in the energy transition.

One of the most significant barriers to the widespread adoption of prosumer models is the complexity of existing legal and regulatory frameworks. In many countries, energy markets have historically been built around centralized systems, where large utility companies are responsible for energy generation, transmission, and distribution. This centralization has resulted in regulations that favor traditional models of energy production and consumption, creating challenges for prosumers who seek to generate, manage, and sell their own energy.

For example, the process of connecting renewable energy systems to the grid can be legally complex. Many regions have outdated grid access rules that were designed with large, centralized power plants in mind and may not accommodate small-scale, decentralized energy generation. Prosumers often face lengthy permitting processes, high connection fees, or unclear guidelines for grid integration, making it difficult for them to participate in the energy market. Furthermore, regulations governing the sale of excess energy back to the grid, such as net metering policies, vary widely between regions and can significantly impact the financial viability of prosumer models. In some areas, prosumers are not compensated fairly for the energy they contribute, while in others, the legal framework may not allow for energy sharing or trading at all.

To overcome these regulatory challenges, policymakers need to modernize energy laws to reflect the realities of decentralized energy systems. This includes revising grid access rules to facilitate the integration of small-scale renewable energy systems and creating clear, standardized procedures for connecting prosumers to the grid. Additionally, policymakers can implement net metering policies or feed-in tariffs that provide fair compensation for prosumers, ensuring that they are rewarded for their contributions to the grid. Developing clear and consistent regulatory frameworks for prosumers will reduce the uncertainty surrounding investment in renewable energy technologies and encourage more widespread adoption.

Political resistance to the energy transition is another significant barrier to the growth of prosumer models. Energy policy is often influenced by entrenched interests, such as fossil fuel industries, which have historically played a dominant role in many national economies. In regions where fossil fuels remain a significant source of energy and revenue, there may be strong political resistance to policies that promote renewable energy or decentralized energy systems. This resistance can manifest in the form of lobbying from fossil fuel companies, opposition from political parties that favor traditional energy sources, or the slow pace of policy reform due to vested interests.

Additionally, political resistance can stem from concerns about the potential economic and social disruptions associated with the energy transition. For example, policymakers may be hesitant to support prosumer models due to fears about job losses in traditional energy sectors or the impact on existing utility companies. In some cases, utility companies may actively lobby against prosumer-friendly policies, as decentralized energy systems could undermine their business models and profitability. This dynamic can lead to a lack of political will to support prosumer-friendly policies, further delaying the adoption of renewable energy technologies and the decentralization of energy production.

To overcome political resistance, it is crucial to build broad coalitions that support the energy transition. This includes engaging stakeholders across the political spectrum, including policymakers, utilities, and labor unions, to develop policies that create a just and equitable transition for all involved. For example, the development of policies that include just transition frameworks can help address concerns about job displacement by supporting retraining programs and investments in new industries, such as renewable energy and energy efficiency. By demonstrating that renewable energy policies can create jobs, reduce energy costs, and increase energy security, it is possible to build a broader base of support for prosumer models.

Public pressure and grassroots movements can also play an important role in overcoming political resistance. As more individuals and communities become engaged in the energy transition, they can advocate for policies that support prosumer participation. Public awareness campaigns that highlight the benefits of prosumer models—such as lower energy costs, increased energy independence, and environmental sustainability—can help shift public opinion and create political momentum for change. Additionally, international climate agreements and commitments, such as the Paris Agreement, can serve as a catalyst for change, encouraging governments to adopt more ambitious renewable energy policies and support the role of prosumers in achieving climate targets.

In addition to overcoming political resistance, creating supportive regulatory environments is essential for the growth of prosumer models. This includes establishing incentives and subsidies that lower the financial barriers to entry for prosumers, as well as creating regulations that enable the efficient integration of renewable energy technologies into the grid. Governments can also provide support for research and development in energy storage, smart grids, and other technologies that facilitate the integration of decentralized energy systems.

At the same time, policymakers should work to ensure that the benefits of prosumer participation are distributed equitably. This means ensuring that low-income households and underserved communities have access to renewable energy technologies and can participate in the energy transition. Community energy projects, for example, can help democratize access to renewable energy by allowing multiple stakeholders to invest in and benefit from shared renewable energy resources.

Chapter 9: The Path Forward for Energy Prosumers

As the world continues its transition to a more sustainable, decentralized energy system, the role of energy prosumers will become increasingly critical in shaping the future of energy production, consumption, and distribution. This chapter explores the path forward for energy prosumers, focusing on the key developments, opportunities, and strategies that will enable their continued growth and success. It examines how technological advancements, evolving policy frameworks, and societal shifts can further empower prosumers to contribute to a clean energy future. Additionally, the chapter highlights the importance of creating inclusive, equitable systems that ensure all communities can participate in and benefit from the energy transition. By exploring these emerging opportunities and addressing the challenges that remain, this chapter outlines the steps needed to unlock the full potential of prosumers in building a sustainable, resilient, and decentralized energy landscape.

9.1. Strategies for Scaling Prosumption

As the adoption of prosumer models grows, scaling these initiatives to reach a broader population is essential for accelerating the transition to decentralized, renewable energy systems. For scaling to be successful, both government policy and business strategies must align to create an enabling environment that encourages widespread prosumer participation. This section outlines key policy recommendations for governments and business strategies for engaging prosumers to ensure that the growth of prosumer models is inclusive, efficient, and sustainable.

Governments play a critical role in creating the framework for scaling prosumer models. To support the growth of prosumption, governments must introduce and implement policies that lower financial and technical barriers while promoting equitable access to renewable energy technologies. One of the most important steps is the introduction of clear, stable, and supportive regulatory frameworks. This includes revising existing regulations to facilitate grid access for prosumers and ensuring that the integration of small-scale renewable energy systems into the grid is simple and cost-effective. Streamlining permitting processes, reducing connection fees, and providing clear guidelines for interconnection will help reduce the administrative burden on prosumers and make it easier for individuals and communities to participate.

Governments can also promote prosumption by providing financial incentives such as tax credits, subsidies, or low-interest loans for the installation of renewable energy systems. These incentives help reduce the high upfront costs of solar panels, wind turbines, and energy storage systems, making renewable energy more accessible to a broader range of households and businesses. Additionally, programs like feed-in tariffs and net metering can provide fair compensation for prosumers, ensuring they are rewarded for the energy they contribute to the grid. By ensuring fair pricing and compensation for energy generation, governments can create a financial incentive for prosumers to continue investing in renewable energy technologies.

Another key policy recommendation is to support the development of smart grids and energy storage systems that enable efficient energy distribution and management. These technologies allow prosumers to store excess energy for later use or sell it back to the grid, ensuring that renewable energy is used efficiently and grid stability is maintained. Investment in infrastructure, such as advanced metering systems, can provide real-time data for both prosumers and grid operators, enabling better decision-making and more effective integration of decentralized energy sources.

Finally, governments should ensure that policies prioritize equity and inclusivity in the energy transition. This includes ensuring that low-income households and underserved communities have access to renewable energy technologies and can participate in prosumer models. Community-based energy projects, which allow multiple participants to share the benefits of renewable energy, can help democratize access and ensure that the energy transition does not leave vulnerable populations behind.

For businesses, engaging prosumers requires a combination of innovative products, services, and outreach efforts that align with the values and needs of consumers. One key strategy for businesses is to offer customizable and affordable energy solutions that cater to different customer segments, including homeowners, small businesses, and communities. By providing flexible financing options, such as subscription-based models, leasing arrangements, or pay-as-you-go services, businesses can lower the barriers to entry for prosumers and make renewable energy more accessible to a wide range of consumers.

Businesses should also focus on offering integrated energy solutions that combine renewable energy generation, energy storage, and energy management systems in one package. This could include offering smart home systems that help prosumers optimize energy consumption, monitor energy production and usage, and control devices remotely. The integration of energy storage with renewable energy systems is crucial for maximizing energy independence and ensuring reliable energy supply, particularly in areas where grid access may be unreliable.

Another strategy for businesses is to develop platforms for peer-to-peer energy trading, enabling prosumers to sell excess energy directly to others within their community or region. These platforms leverage blockchain and other digital technologies to facilitate secure, transparent energy transactions, empowering prosumers to participate more actively in energy markets and increase the financial benefits of their renewable energy systems. By creating such platforms, businesses can build a more decentralized energy market that supports prosumers and promotes the efficient use of renewable energy.

Finally, businesses must invest in education and outreach to increase consumer awareness of the benefits of prosumption and renewable energy adoption. By providing clear, accessible information about the environmental, economic, and technical advantages of prosumer models, businesses can encourage more people to become involved in the energy transition. Offering customer support services, including installation, maintenance, and troubleshooting, can also help alleviate concerns and make renewable energy technologies more approachable for first-time users.

9.2. Technological Innovations

The future of energy prosumption is largely shaped by ongoing technological innovations that are making renewable energy systems more efficient, affordable, and accessible. As renewable energy technologies continue to advance, prosumers are presented with new opportunities to generate, store, and manage energy more effectively. This section explores the future prospects for renewable energy technologies, with a focus on innovations in energy storage and grid management, which are essential to scaling prosumer models and ensuring the integration of decentralized energy systems.

Renewable energy technologies have experienced significant improvements over the past decade, and future advancements promise to further enhance their efficiency and affordability. Solar power, for example, has already seen a drastic reduction in costs, with the price of solar panels falling by over 80% since 2010. In the future, continued innovations in PV materials and manufacturing processes are expected to make solar energy even more cost-competitive. One promising development is bifacial solar panels, which can capture sunlight from both sides of the panel, increasing energy production without requiring additional space. Perovskite solar cells, another emerging technology, are expected to offer higher efficiency rates at lower costs compared to traditional silicon-based panels, providing new opportunities for prosumers to generate renewable energy at home or in communities.

Wind energy is also likely to see continued technological progress, with advancements in offshore wind farms and small-scale wind turbines. Offshore wind farms have the potential to generate large amounts of energy due to higher and more consistent wind speeds, and advancements in turbine design are expected to improve energy output while reducing costs. For prosumers, small-scale wind turbines offer an opportunity to harness renewable energy in areas with suitable wind conditions, making it a viable option for decentralized energy generation.

Other renewable technologies, such as biomass, hydropower, and geothermal energy, are also poised to benefit from ongoing innovations that increase their efficiency and environmental sustainability. These technologies are particularly well-suited to specific geographical regions and can complement solar and wind energy systems in a prosumer-driven energy model. The diversification of renewable energy sources ensures that prosumers can choose the most suitable technology based on their location, resource availability, and energy needs.

Energy storage and grid management are crucial components for the widespread adoption of prosumer models. As more prosumers generate renewable energy, efficient storage and management systems are needed to ensure that excess energy can be stored and used when production is low. Advances in battery storage technologies are expected to play a key role in this regard. The development of more efficient, cost-effective, and longer-lasting batteries is essential for storing renewable energy at the individual and community levels.

Solid-state batteries are one such innovation that holds significant promise for energy storage. These batteries are safer, more energy-dense, and longer-lasting than traditional lithium-ion batteries, which are commonly used in residential energy storage systems. With improved storage capacity, prosumers can store more energy for later use, reducing reliance on the grid during periods of low renewable energy production. Furthermore, advances in flow batteries, which store energy in liquid electrolytes, are being explored as an alternative to traditional battery technologies for larger-scale storage solutions.

In addition to storage innovations, smart grids are crucial for managing the flow of energy between prosumers, the grid, and utility companies. Smart grids use digital communication technologies to monitor energy demand and supply in real time, enabling grid operators to make more informed decisions about energy distribution. Smart grids allow for demand-side management, where energy use can be adjusted based on supply conditions, improving efficiency and reducing strain on the grid. For prosumers, smart grids enable the seamless integration of renewable energy systems with the grid, ensuring that energy is efficiently distributed and that excess energy can be sold back to the grid or shared with other prosumers.

The development of microgrids is another important innovation in grid management. Microgrids are localized networks that can operate independently or in conjunction with the larger grid, allowing for greater energy resilience and security. In areas prone to power outages or where grid infrastructure is limited, microgrids can provide a reliable source of energy by integrating local renewable energy sources, such as solar, wind, and battery storage. For prosumers, microgrids offer an opportunity to share energy with neighboring homes or businesses, creating a more decentralized and flexible energy system.

Finally, AI and machine learning are increasingly being used to optimize energy production, consumption, and storage. AI can analyze real-time data from renewable energy systems, energy storage devices, and the grid to predict energy demand and supply fluctuations, helping to ensure that energy is used efficiently and that excess energy is stored or distributed when needed. These technologies help improve the overall performance and integration of renewable energy systems, making prosumer models more viable and sustainable in the long term.

9.3. Collaboration and Partnerships

The future of energy prosumption relies heavily on the collaboration between various stakeholders, including governments, businesses, non-governmental organizations, and communities. Public-private partnerships (PPPs) and international collaboration offer valuable opportunities for scaling prosumer models and accelerating the transition to decentralized, renewable energy systems. These partnerships can provide the resources, expertise, and policy support needed to overcome the barriers to prosumer adoption and ensure that renewable energy is accessible to a broad range of participants. This section explores the role of public-private partnerships in fostering prosumption and the opportunities for international collaboration in advancing the energy transition.

Public-private partnerships play a vital role in scaling prosumer models by combining the strengths of both the public and private sectors. Governments have the policy-making authority and the ability to provide incentives and support for renewable energy adoption, while private companies possess the technological expertise and resources needed to develop and deploy energy systems. When these sectors collaborate, they can create a favorable environment for prosumers to invest in renewable energy technologies and integrate them into the broader energy system.

One key role of PPPs in fostering prosumption is the development and implementation of financial incentives. Governments can provide subsidies, tax credits, or low-interest loans to encourage the adoption of renewable energy systems by prosumers. However, these incentives are often insufficient on their own without the involvement of the private sector to provide affordable technologies and financing options. Through PPPs, governments can work with private companies to develop innovative financial products, such as pay-as-you-go solar systems or community-based energy financing models, which reduce the financial burden on prosumers and make renewable energy systems more accessible.

PPPs also facilitate the development of infrastructure that supports prosumer models, such as smart grids, energy storage systems, and microgrids. These technologies enable the integration of distributed renewable energy sources, like solar and wind, into the existing energy infrastructure, ensuring that prosumers can generate, store, and manage energy effectively. Governments can provide the policy framework and funding for these infrastructure projects, while private companies can contribute the technological expertise and resources needed to implement them at scale. Through collaboration, these projects can be developed more efficiently, benefiting both prosumers and the broader energy system.

Another key area where PPPs can foster prosumption is in research and development (R&D). The continued advancement of renewable energy technologies, energy storage systems, and smart grid solutions is crucial to scaling prosumer models and making them more efficient and cost-effective. Governments and private companies can collaborate on R&D initiatives to develop next-generation technologies that reduce costs, improve performance, and enhance the integration of renewable energy into decentralized systems. Public funding for R&D can be combined with private sector innovation and expertise to accelerate the commercialization of new technologies, making them more widely available to prosumers.

The transition to renewable energy is a global challenge, and international collaboration is essential for ensuring that prosumer models can be scaled and implemented effectively across borders. While each country may have its own specific energy needs and priorities, the shared goals of reducing carbon emissions, increasing energy security, and promoting sustainable development create opportunities for countries to collaborate and exchange knowledge, technologies, and best practices.

One area where international collaboration is particularly valuable is in the standardization of policies and technologies. Many countries are at different stages of the energy transition, and as a result, there is a lack of consistency in the regulatory frameworks that support prosumer models. By collaborating on the development of international standards for grid integration, energy storage, and prosumer compensation, countries can create a more harmonized global energy market. This would reduce the complexity and cost of implementing prosumer systems and create a more level playing field for businesses and consumers alike. International organizations such as the International Energy Agency (IEA) and the International Renewable Energy Agency (IRENA) play a key role in fostering collaboration and standardization, helping countries align their efforts and share knowledge.

Cross-border trade of renewable energy is another area where international collaboration can benefit prosumers. As more countries and regions adopt decentralized energy systems, there will be increasing opportunities for prosumers to trade energy across borders. For example, if one region is experiencing excess solar or wind generation, energy could be traded with neighboring regions that may be experiencing higher demand. International collaboration on grid infrastructure and market mechanisms will be essential to facilitating cross-border energy trade and enabling prosumers to benefit from regional energy surpluses. Collaborative efforts can also help ensure that energy generated in one country can be used to meet the needs of another, reducing energy insecurity and promoting regional cooperation.

Additionally, international collaboration can support the transfer of technology and capacity building in developing countries. Many nations still lack the resources and expertise needed to deploy renewable energy technologies at scale. By fostering partnerships between developed and developing countries, knowledge and technology can be shared to help accelerate the adoption of prosumer models in emerging markets. This collaboration can include providing access to financing for renewable energy projects, offering technical training, and supporting local businesses in the energy sector. By ensuring that all countries can participate in the energy transition, international collaboration can help create a more equitable and inclusive global energy system.

Finally, climate change mitigation is another area where international collaboration can enhance the effectiveness of prosumer models. As countries work toward achieving their climate targets under agreements such as the Paris Agreement, collaboration on prosumer policies and technologies can contribute to global emissions reductions. By sharing best practices and aligning renewable energy goals, countries can work together to accelerate the adoption of decentralized energy systems and ensure that prosumers play a key role in meeting international climate commitments.

9.4. Vision for a Prosumer-Driven Future

As the global energy landscape continues to evolve, a vision of a decentralized, sustainable energy system emerges, where individuals and communities actively contribute to energy generation, storage, and management. In such a system, energy prosumers are not just passive consumers of electricity but active participants in the energy market, helping to reshape the way energy is produced and consumed. This vision of a prosumer-driven future is underpinned by advancements in renewable energy technologies, innovative energy management systems, and supportive regulatory frameworks. Additionally, the integration of prosumers into circular economy systems plays a crucial role in creating a more sustainable, resilient, and equitable energy system.

A decentralized energy system offers the promise of greater energy independence, resilience, and sustainability. In this vision, energy is generated not just by large, centralized power plants but by millions of small-scale, distributed renewable energy systems owned by prosumers. These systems—ranging from rooftop solar panels and small wind turbines to community-based microgrids and energy storage solutions—allow individuals and communities to take control of their energy needs, reducing reliance on traditional, fossil-fuel-based power sources.

In a decentralized energy landscape, renewable energy sources such as solar, wind, and hydro play a dominant role in meeting global energy demand. These energy sources are abundant, clean, and increasingly affordable, making them the foundation of the energy system. With the continued decline in the cost of renewable technologies, along with advancements in energy storage, prosumers can generate and store their own energy with greater ease and efficiency. This shift enables households and businesses to reduce their dependence on the grid, allowing them to produce their own electricity when conditions are favorable and store surplus energy for use when production is low.

The integration of smart grids and energy management systems ensures that this decentralized energy production can be seamlessly coordinated with the broader grid. Smart grids, equipped with advanced sensors and digital communication technologies, allow for real-time monitoring and management of energy flows between prosumers, the grid, and utility companies. These systems ensure that energy is distributed efficiently, even in the context of fluctuating supply and demand. For prosumers, smart grids provide the flexibility to share excess energy with the grid or other prosumers, further supporting the decentralization of the energy market.

This decentralized approach to energy production and consumption is not only more sustainable but also more resilient. By diversifying the sources of energy generation and incorporating local storage solutions, decentralized systems are less vulnerable to supply disruptions, whether from natural disasters, grid failures, or geopolitical events. In a prosumer-driven future, the energy system is more adaptable and capable of maintaining service even in the face of challenges.

Integration of Prosumers in Circular Economy Systems

A prosumer-driven future also aligns closely with the principles of the circular economy, which seeks to minimize waste, maximize resource efficiency, and create closed-loop systems where products and materials are reused and recycled. In the context of energy, a circular economy approach involves not only the generation of renewable energy by prosumers but also the reuse and recycling of materials, the reduction of energy consumption, and the efficient management of energy resources across their entire life cycle.

One of the key ways prosumers can contribute to a circular economy is by integrating renewable energy production with energy storage systems. As prosumers generate more energy than they need at certain times, the excess energy can be stored in batteries or energy storage devices for later use. This reduces the need for additional energy generation from non-renewable sources and ensures that the energy generated is used more efficiently. Furthermore, the energy storage systems themselves can be designed for long-term durability and recyclability, minimizing waste and contributing to a more sustainable energy system.

Prosumers also have the opportunity to contribute to the circular economy through the reuse and recycling of energy systems. As renewable energy technologies, such as solar panels and wind turbines, reach the end of their operational life, the materials used in these systems—such as metals, glass, and plastics—can be repurposed or recycled to create new products or systems. This reduces the environmental impact of these technologies and helps ensure that the materials used in energy generation are not discarded but are instead reintegrated into the economy, creating a more sustainable cycle of production and consumption.

In a circular energy system, prosumers also play a role in energy efficiency. By adopting energy-efficient appliances, improving building insulation, and optimizing energy consumption with smart home systems, prosumers can reduce their overall energy demand. This approach not only helps lower energy costs but also reduces the strain on the broader energy system, making it more efficient and sustainable. Additionally, by generating energy locally and using it efficiently, prosumers can minimize the need for energy transport, which is associated with significant energy losses.

The integration of prosumers into circular economy systems can extend beyond individual households and businesses. For example, community-based energy projects allow groups of prosumers to collectively manage energy resources, share energy production, and optimize energy use. These projects can also incorporate waste-to-energy technologies, where organic waste is converted into biogas or other forms of renewable energy, further closing the loop and reducing waste in the community.

Furthermore, circular economy principles can be applied to the design and manufacture of energy technologies themselves. For instance, renewable energy systems can be designed for easy disassembly and recycling, ensuring that components are reused or repurposed at the end of their lifespan. Businesses that manufacture renewable energy systems can adopt circular economy models in their supply chains, using sustainably sourced materials and minimizing waste in production processes.

Conclusion

As the world faces the pressing challenges of climate change, resource depletion, and energy inequality, the role of energy prosumers in shaping a sustainable, decentralized energy future has never been more critical. This conclusion synthesizes the key insights discussed throughout the book, reflecting on the transformative potential of prosumer models and the collective action needed to foster their growth. By examining the technological, economic, social, and policy challenges that must be addressed, this chapter highlights the strategies and pathways that can help scale prosumer participation, create a fair and inclusive energy system, and contribute to global climate goals. The journey toward a prosumer-driven energy future requires continued innovation, collaboration, and commitment to sustainable development, ensuring that all communities, regardless of their location or economic status, can play an active role in the energy transition.

Summary of the Transformative Role of Energy Prosumers

Energy prosumers are playing an increasingly transformative role in the global energy transition. By generating, managing, and consuming their own energy, prosumers are shifting the traditional energy paradigm from a centralized system controlled by large utilities to a more decentralized, renewable, and participatory model. This change not only empowers individuals and communities to take control of their energy needs but also contributes to the reduction of greenhouse gas emissions, making prosumers vital actors in the effort to combat climate change.

Prosumers contribute to a more sustainable energy system by adopting renewable energy technologies, such as solar panels and wind turbines, which reduce reliance on fossil fuels. Their participation in decentralized energy production also promotes energy security and resilience, as prosumers generate energy locally and reduce their dependence on centralized power sources. Additionally, innovations in energy storage, smart grids, and digital platforms further enhance the efficiency and integration of renewable energy, enabling prosumers to store surplus energy and share it with the grid or other users.

Beyond environmental and technical contributions, prosumers also help democratize energy access. By reducing energy costs, increasing energy independence, and creating new economic opportunities, prosumer models have the potential to make energy more affordable and equitable, particularly for underserved and remote communities.

Overall, the rise of energy prosumers represents a critical step toward a decentralized, sustainable, and resilient energy future. Their transformative role extends beyond mere participation, as they actively shape energy markets, foster innovation, and contribute to the global goal of reducing carbon emissions and achieving sustainability.

The importance of Collaboration and Innovation in Overcoming Challenges

Collaboration and innovation are essential to overcoming the challenges that energy prosumers face in transitioning to a decentralized, sustainable energy system. As the adoption of prosumer models expands, technical, economic, social, and regulatory barriers must be addressed collectively to ensure a successful energy transition. Collaboration between governments, businesses, communities, and international organizations is key to creating the supportive policies, infrastructure, and financing mechanisms needed to scale prosumer participation. Public-private partnerships, for example, can combine the strengths of both sectors to develop solutions that foster greater prosumer engagement and expand access to renewable energy technologies.

Innovation plays a crucial role in overcoming these challenges by driving the development of new technologies and systems that enhance energy efficiency and integration. Innovations in renewable energy technologies, such as more efficient solar panels and advanced energy storage systems, make renewable energy more affordable and accessible for prosumers. Furthermore, advancements in smart grids, IoT systems, and blockchain enable more efficient energy management, allowing prosumers to better monitor, store, and share energy.

Addressing barriers such as high upfront costs, complex regulations, and social resistance requires a commitment to both collaborative efforts and innovative solutions. For instance, financial products and incentives can be tailored to encourage prosumer adoption, while policy reforms can be introduced to support equitable access to energy. Ultimately, by fostering collaboration and embracing innovation, the energy transition can be accelerated, making prosumer-driven energy systems a key part of the future of sustainable, decentralized energy.

Final Thoughts on the Future of the Energy Landscape Driven by Prosumers

The future of the energy landscape is undeniably shaped by the growing role of energy prosumers—individuals, businesses, and communities who generate, manage, and consume their own energy. As the world moves toward more sustainable and decentralized energy systems, prosumers are expected to become increasingly central in this transformation. The shift from centralized, fossil-fuel-based energy production to decentralized, renewable energy generation offers substantial environmental, economic, and social benefits, with prosumers at the forefront of this change.

The environmental impact of prosumers is perhaps the most significant driver of this shift. By generating energy from renewable sources such as solar, wind, and biomass, prosumers reduce their reliance on carbon-intensive fossil fuels, directly contributing to the reduction of greenhouse gas emissions. As more prosumers join the energy transition, the cumulative effect can be profound, supporting global climate goals and enhancing energy security. Prosumers help diversify the energy mix, which in turn strengthens the resilience of energy systems by decreasing their vulnerability to external shocks such as geopolitical tensions, natural disasters, or economic disruptions.

Economically, the role of prosumers presents new opportunities. As more individuals and communities generate their own energy, they reduce their dependence on traditional utility services and lower their energy costs. Furthermore, the economic benefits extend beyond cost savings; prosumers can also participate in local energy markets, potentially earning income by selling excess energy back to the grid or sharing it with other consumers. This decentralized model encourages innovation in financing options and technologies, making renewable energy systems more affordable and accessible, especially for underserved or rural populations.

Socially, prosumers contribute to a more equitable energy system by enabling greater energy access and fostering a sense of empowerment within communities. The shift toward prosumer-driven energy systems enables individuals and businesses to take control of their energy needs, reducing energy poverty and allowing communities to become more self-sufficient. In addition, prosumer models encourage community collaboration, such as through shared solar projects or cooperative wind farms, where local residents can collectively benefit from renewable energy production and increase social cohesion.

However, for the full potential of prosumer-driven energy systems to be realized, there are challenges to overcome. Issues related to the high upfront costs of renewable energy technologies, regulatory barriers, and technical limitations such as grid integration and intermittency need to be addressed. Collaboration between governments, businesses, and international organizations will be crucial in overcoming these barriers. Governments must provide clear policies, financial incentives, and regulatory frameworks that support prosumer participation while ensuring a level playing field. Businesses can drive innovation in renewable energy technologies, storage solutions, and digital platforms, making them more accessible and cost-effective for consumers. International collaboration will be key to sharing knowledge, standardizing policies, and developing shared energy markets.

Technological advancements will also play a pivotal role in the future of the energy landscape. The continued development of efficient renewable energy technologies, advanced energy storage solutions, smart grids, and energy management systems will make it easier for prosumers to generate, store, and distribute energy. These innovations will address issues of intermittency, improve grid stability, and reduce energy waste, allowing prosumers to contribute more effectively to the overall energy system.

Ultimately, the future of energy systems driven by prosumers will be characterized by greater sustainability, resilience, and equity. As more individuals and communities participate in the generation and management of renewable energy, the global energy landscape will shift towards more localized, decentralized models. This transition will not only support climate goals but also create economic opportunities and foster social empowerment, making renewable energy a more inclusive and accessible resource for all. The path forward requires continued collaboration, innovation, and commitment to creating a sustainable energy future for generations to come.

www.ingramcontent.com/pod-product-compliance
Lightning Source LLC
Chambersburg PA
CBHW071606200326
41519CB00021BB/6887